THE BOROWITZ REPORT

The Big Book of Shockers

ANDY BOROWITZ

SIMON & SCHUSTER PAPERBACKS

NEW YORK   LONDON   TORONTO   SYDNEY

SIMON & SCHUSTER PAPERBACKS
Rockefeller Center
1230 Avenue of the Americas
New York, NY 10020

Copyright © 2004 by Andy Borowitz
All rights reserved, including the right of
reproduction in whole or in part in any form.

First Simon & Schuster paperback edition 2004

SIMON & SCHUSTER PAPERBACKS and colophon are registered trademarks
of Simon & Schuster, Inc.

For information about special discounts for bulk purchases,
please contact Simon & Schuster Special Sales:
1-800-456-6798 or business@simonandschuster.com.

Designed by Charles Kreloff

All photos courtesy of Getty Images

Manufactured in the United States of America

1   3   5   7   9   10   8   6   4   2

Library of Congress Cataloging-in-Publication Data
Borowitz, Andy.
The Borowitz report: the big book of shockers/Andy Borowitz.
p. cm.
1. American wit and humor. I. Title.
PN6165.B67   2004
814'.6—dc22   2004052470

ISBN 0-7432-6277-8

AXIS OF EVIL

Kim JONG IL, CHAIRMAN

Dear Imperialist Stooges:

Being President of North Korea and Chairman of the Axis of Evil is no day at the beach. Sometimes when I tell people that, they think I'm just bellyaching. Well, there's only one thing to do with people who accuse you of bellyaching—execute them on national TV.

Psyche! If you're going to hang with Kim Jong Il, you better get used to my twisted sense of humor. I've often said, you don't have to be crazy to be President of the most evil nation on Earth—but it helps. I'm totally bent, and I encourage the people I work with to act like whack-jobs, too. If I see that one of my aides is walking around with a spent fuel rod up his ass, I know just how to fix his wagon: I execute him on national TV. *Psyche!* I swear, I've got a million of 'em.

Don't get me wrong: I love my job and I wouldn't trade it for any other job in the world, not even a mindless one that pays boatloads of money like Shaquille O'Neal's or Dan Rather's. If I had to make a list of what I like about being President of North Korea, it would go like this: (1) buying nuclear technology from Pakistani scientists; (2) threatening the West with imminent annihilation; and (3) acting "mercurial." And that's just the top three! You don't know how bodacious it is to stand on your balcony and watch 1 million brainwashed soldiers in uniform passing below you with all of those awesome missiles and tanks and shit. I may put on my frowny-face for the cameras—that's a part of my job I like, too—but inside, Kim Jong Il is saying to himself, "Sweet!"

So what *don't* I like about my job? It all comes down to three little words: Axis of Evil. Every time I think about the day I agreed to be Chairman of the AOE, I could practically kick myself! Here's the way it went down: I was at an AOE meeting (it was our annual golf outing in Scottsdale) with Iran and Iraq sometime back in 2002. Someone—I think it might have been that douchebag Saddam Hussein—suggested that I would make a kick-ass Chairman of the Axis. Well, I'd be lying if I said I wasn't flattered. When you've dedicated your whole life to evildoing, there are really only two ultimate dream jobs out there—running the Axis of Evil or a movie studio. So, all-day sucker that I am, I said yes!

Word to the wise: anyone who says that being Chairman of the Axis of Evil is a chance to roll up your sleeves and do lots of evil shit is totally selling you a bill of goods. I'll tell you the truly "evil" part of the Axis of Evil—the paperwork! I thought being put in charge of the AOE would mean I'd be spending most of my time cooking up sinister plots or maybe designing secret underground hideouts and junk, but as it turned out about 99.9999 percent of the job is administrative. Evil my ass—I might as well be running AARP.

To make matters worse, in early 2003 the other AOE members started dropping like flies, leaving yours truly holding the proverbial bag. I remember turning on the TV and seeing all of those statues of Saddam toppling and saying to myself, "Not cool, man. Not cool at all." But Iraq dropping out of the Axis of Evil was a nightmare for me in more ways than one. Not many people outside the AOE knew this, but Saddam Hussein was Chairman of our fucking *Refreshments*

Committee. Now that he was gone, there was no one, I repeat, *no one*, to work on the Axis of Evil's Spring Dance.

Then Iran started talking about letting nuclear inspectors into their country, and I'm like, Excuse me, but when did this become the Axis of Wussies? How come no one sent me that fucking memo, folks? All of a sudden, all kinds of crazy shit was going down (don't get me started on Libya) and I was like totally, *totally* out of the freaking loop.

Which brings me to another thing about my job that I'm not bananas about: when you're dictator of a closed society like North Korea, it's really tough to get access to accurate news and information. Maybe it's the fact that there are no independent newspapers, TV networks or radio stations. Maybe it's because people won't tell you the truth since they're afraid you're going to "shoot the messenger." If there's one thing I've learned, it's this: you shoot a few thousand messengers and it really comes back to haunt you.

But I was determined never to be blindsided by world events again. I gathered together the top officials from North Korea's Ministry of Truth and told them to fan out across the globe and bring back a news and information service that was so accurate, so thorough, so unimpeachable that it would keep me ahead of the curve from now until the end of time (which I've currently penciled in for May 2008). After weeks of scouring the planet for such a news service, they finally came back with one: The Borowitz Report.

From that day on, I haven't gone a day without it. In fact, you could say that the superb, in-depth reporting of The Borowitz Report has turned Mr. Kim Jong Il into something of a news "junkie." Simply put, the news stories one finds in The Borowitz Report day in, day out, can't be found anywhere else. A quick scan of such headlines as OPENLY EPISCOPAL MAN JOINS VILLAGE PEOPLE or BUSH MAY LACK GENE FOR HUMAN SPEECH makes you wonder—where was the rest of the news media when these stories were breaking? But even as I devoured stories like those, it dawned on me that The Borowitz Report was more than just the world's most accurate news service. In showing the world for the treacherous place that it is, The Borowitz Report offered North Korea the information necessary for our very survival!

Springing into action, I collected the most shocking news stories from The Borowitz Report, had them translated into Korean and compiled into a book complete with notes from my own personal "blog." I then forced every man, woman and child in North Korea to buy the book and required them, under penalty of death, to submit to a government-mandated pop quiz on its contents. Within its first week on sale, *The Borowitz Report: The Big Book of Shockers* sold well over ten million copies in North Korea, shooting to number one on our nation's bestseller list and staying there for twenty weeks, until it was finally knocked from its lofty perch by *The South Beach Diet.*

Word of the book's history-making sales figures eventually reached the U.S., where a prominent U.S. publisher quickly snapped up the American rights to the book and translated it from Korean back into English. It is to that publisher, Simon & Schuster, that I dedicate this book. To everyone at S&S, let me just say this: working with an American publisher for the first time can be a scary experience, even for a North Korean dictator, but all of you evildoers made this evildoer feel very much at home.

Peace out,
Kim Jong Il

MAJORITY OF AMERICANS NOW BELIEVE EVIL IS BAD, SURVEY SAYS

Sign that President's Message May Be Getting Through

In an indication that President Bush has been effective in communicating his message to the American people, a new survey released today indicates that a majority of Americans now believe that evil is bad.

Of those responding, 54 percent strongly agreed with the statement "Evil is bad," with 21 percent strongly agreeing with the statement "Evil is very, very bad."

By wide margins, those surveyed also agreed with the statement "Evildoers are bad."

In one of the most persuasive pieces of data in the survey, 87 percent agreed with the statement "Evildoers are bad because they do evil, which is bad."

And a whopping 91 percent agreed with the statement "I really mean it."

The University of Minnesota poll, whose margin of error is plus or minus five percentage points, shows that the President's message about evil, evildoers, and other evil stuff may be taking hold.

However, those responding to the survey still had some difficulty identifying the three members of the "Axis of Evil" whom President Bush identified in his State of the Union speech.

Only 12 percent correctly identified Iran, Iraq, and North Korea, while 23 percent incor-

President Bush's speeches about evil being bad have sent approval ratings for evil tumbling to an all-time low.

rectly named Batman supervillains the Joker, the Riddler, and Catwoman.

In other poll results, 61 percent agreed with the statement "Washington, D.C., is the capital of the USA," and 57 percent correctly identified the number two as the sum of one plus one.

KIM'S BLOG

Most people figure that whenever President Bush talks about "the Axis of Evil" or evildoers or whatnot, that would really piss me off. *Au contraire, homes!* The fact is, every time he says the word "evil" it's just more free publicity for yours truly.

Face it, before Bush was President practically no one had even heard of Kim Jong Il or North Korea or our superscary nuclear weapons program, but thanks to all of his speeches, my brand awareness is now sky-high. In some parts of the world I'm now better known than Vanilla Coke! There's only one word for that: awesome.

I'll tell you something else. Before Bush was elected, I was busting my hump to get publicity—Internet banner ads, radio spots, you name it. I even showed up at the Golden Globes one year with Mary Steenburgen. What did it get me? Nada!

The fact is, nothing gets your name out there faster and better than being called "evil" in a State of the Union address. If there's one thing that bugs me, though, I guess it's this: people can't decide whether to spell my name Kim Jung-Il or Kim *Jong Il*. My publicist says that the whole spelling thing is keeping me from truly breaking out and we've got to clear it up somehow if I want to make it to the cover of *People*. (Everyone knows how to spell "Clooney," she says.) Now I totally understand why Cher and Madonna went the one-name route! I guess when people just start referring to me as "Kim," then I'll know I've arrived.

OSAMA'S WIFE, DEBBIE BIN LADEN, SPEAKS OUT

Rips Terror-Hubby in Exclusive Chat

Question: What's worse than being the world's most wanted man, hunted by U.S. Special Operations Forces while bunker-busting missiles jangle your nerves morning, noon and night?

Answer: Being trapped in a one-room cave with four really pissed-off wives.

Much has been written and said about Osama bin Laden, the evildoer, but relatively little is known about Osama bin Laden, the henpecked husband.

Until now.

Sources close to the bin Laden household say that there is "trouble in paradise," and a recent exclusive interview with one of Osama's four wives, Debbie bin Laden, appears to bear this out.

"The world knows how evil Osama is," Debbie bin Laden says. "What they don't know is how cheap he is."

The exclusive Debbie bin Laden interview appears in the new issue of *Angry People*, a popular Kandahar magazine.

In it, Debbie bin Laden says that "the day the allied bombers knocked out all of the power plants in Kandahar was the happiest day in Osama's life, because he knew it would bring down our electric bill."

Her husband is so cheap, Debbie bin Laden says, that he allegedly told the Taliban to ban all movies "just so he wouldn't have to take us to any."

"It's no coincidence that they banned dinner and dancing, too," Mrs. bin Laden says.

"His idea of a good time is popping one of those spooky propaganda videos he made into the VCR," claims Debbie bin Laden. "How many times can you watch him going 'Death to America'? That gets old real fast."

All in all, the picture Debbie bin Laden paints of life with her notorious husband falls far short of the glamour she and her fellow wives—Rhonda bin Laden, Barb bin Laden, and Kelly bin Laden—thought they were marrying into.

"I don't want people to think we're a bunch of gold-diggers or anything," Debbie says. "But when you marry a millionaire, you don't think you're going to spend the rest of your life crouching in a mud hut."

Osama bin Laden's wife Debbie bin Laden (left) organizes a rally of angry bin Laden wives in a suburb of Kandahar.

CLINTON DELIVERS FIRST "STATE OF CHAPPAQUA" ADDRESS

Five-Hour Speech Finally Ends When Neighbors Call Police

Former President Bill Clinton, hoping to establish an annual tradition for his retirement years, delivered his first "State of Chappaqua" address tonight from the roof of his suburban home.

The President's trademark hoarse voice could be heard booming throughout the leafy community, amplified by a handheld megaphone the former President had purchased at Radio Shack earlier in the day.

The wide-ranging speech, which covered such topics as Chappaqua's schools, traffic and commerce lasted five hours and threatened to continue well into the wee hours of the morning.

But angry neighbors flooded the police with calls, demanding that the authorities tell the former President to stop speaking at once.

Chappaqua residents appeared dismayed and exasperated by the former President's long-winded address, which several neighbors described as the most tedious speech they had ever heard.

"When he first moved here and started driving around with 'Do You Think I'm Sexy?' blasting from his car stereo, I thought it couldn't get any worse than that," said Carl Bolton, a neighbor of the former President's. "Now I know that it can—much worse."

Former President Bill Clinton poses with his wife, Sen. Hillary Clinton (D-N.Y.), just hours before Chappaqua police forced him to stop talking.

Other residents were more sympathetic with the plight of the former President, who has seemed restless of late in this sleepy New York hamlet.

"You have to feel sorry for him," said resident Ben Tarkow. "He's really seemed bummed out ever since his wife made him take down that telescope."

MOST BASEBALL PLAYERS ON STEROIDS AND THE REST ARE GAY

Pagan Human Sacrifice Rituals "Widespread" in Nation's Pastime, Former Player Says

Baseball was rocked by controversy again today as a former player charged that a majority of baseball players use steroids and the rest are gay.

The former player spoke on condition of anonymity because, in his words, "Dudes on steroids can really kick your ass."

Even as Major League Baseball officials refused to comment on the player's claims, another unnamed player came forward to say that performance-enhancing human sacrifice rituals were "widespread" in major league locker rooms.

The unnamed player spoke on condition of anonymity for fear of being burned alive on a pagan pyre.

But he indicated that the practice of human sacrifice was common throughout baseball, especially in the National League Central.

Most of the human sacrifice ceremonies in baseball are in supplication to Norse deities such as Odin or Thor, the unnamed player said.

Few baseball players were willing to comment on the heathen ritual controversy, but one player, speaking on condition of anonymity, said he thought that the issue was "no big deal."

"If a guy is hitting the ball well, I don't think the fans care if he's burning human flesh for Odin when he's off the field," the unnamed player said.

Further roiling the baseball world today were the accusations of yet another unnamed player, who charged that well over half the players in Major League Baseball have no names.

"I'm not going to name names," the unnamed player said. "They know who they are."

New York Yankees fans are dismayed to learn that all of their favorite players are either using steroids or gay.

QUEEN ELIZABETH CAUGHT SMOKING POT

In Latest Royal Bust, Stoned Sovereign Found with Giant Spliff

In the latest drug scandal to hit the British royal family, Queen Elizabeth II was found smoking a gigantic marijuana "spliff" in a garden shed behind Buckingham Palace today.

A cloud of smoke from the enormous joint was spotted rising above the palace by eagle-eyed tourists who were waiting to see the Changing of the Guard, a popular London tourist attraction.

Fearing that the garden shed was on fire, palace guards burst into the small outbuilding and found the British sovereign puffing on the enormous spliff while listening to a boom box playing last year's surprise hit "Because I Got High" by the rapper Afroman.

The British tabloids had a field day with the royal family's latest drugscapade.

A few days after running headlines that screamed HARRY POTHEAD! referring to Prince Harry's own unfortunate dope-smoking woes, the London tabs churned out headers like HIGH COURT! and QE2 TRIP!

Making matters worse for the increasingly stoned Windsors was the discovery on palace grounds, late Tuesday evening, of a psychedelic marijuana "bong" belonging to the Queen Mother.

Fearing that public opinion could quickly

Observers said that Queen Elizabeth II had an "attack of the giggles and the munchies" in a meeting with burn victims in a London hospital.

turn against the pot-addled royals, Prince Charles issued a statement to the nation warning of the dangers of drug use.

"Taking drugs results in indolence, idleness, and a lifetime on public assistance," Charles said. "The drug-taker finds herself incapable of little more than attending ceremonial receptions, presiding over the opening of new hospitals, and meddling in her children's marriages."

Minutes after Charles' statement was released, Queen Elizabeth issued a statement of her own.

"We fundamentally believe that the Prince is entitled to his opinions," the Queen's statement read. "But if he gets anywhere near our stash, we are going to cut him."

KIM'S BLOG

When people start flapping their gums about who's the biggest threat in the world today, yours truly usually finds his name at or near the top of the list. That's too bad, because for my money the single most dangerous person on the planet is none other than Queen Elizabeth II of England.

People go on and on about how scary I am in my sunglasses and all, but have you taken a good look at Old Prune Face lately? Her hats alone are enough to terrify me, and I don't scare easy. But even if QE2 somehow got an extreme fashion makeover (which I would personally pay for), she would still be the scariest person in the world, in my book.

Why? Well, let me drop some knowledge on you. I've done a little statistical analysis, and if you add up the IQ's of every member of Queen Elizabeth's family and then take the average, the number you'll wind up with will be roughly half that of your average NHL goalie.

Scared yet? Then consider this: these morons are running a country that has nuclear weapons! You wonder why I stay up half the night reprocessing spent fuel rods. Dude, it's called self-defense!

U.S. ISSUES LIST OF 5,000 BAD THINGS THAT MIGHT HAPPEN SOMEDAY

Falling Pianos Top List of Hypothetical Bad Things

Stung by recent criticism that it has been behind the curve on terror threats, the U.S. government today released an alphabetized list of 5,000 bad things that, in the words of the document, "might happen today, tomorrow, next week, next month, or next year."

The document, published in an eight-pound hardcover book, has been called the single scariest government publication since the Starr Report.

It is also available in a books-on-tape version, with readers John Ashcroft, Dick Cheney, Donald H. Rumsfeld and Tom Ridge giving spooky renditions of the lengthy list of bad things.

While some of the bad things on the list are familiar, some are new, including a possible al-Qaeda plot to rent apartments, rent pianos, and then push the pianos out of the apartment windows.

When asked about the piano plot, White House press secretary Scott McClellan hedged a bit, saying that intelligence agents eavesdropping on al-Qaeda radio communications could not definitively tell if they were saying "pianos" or "peonies."

"They're not as dangerous as pianos, of course, but peonies can still do a lot of harm," Mr. McClellan said.

Mr. McClellan also said that it is possible that al-Qaeda meant they were planning to push live ponies out of apartment windows.

"If they didn't mean pianos or peonies but actually meant ponies, God help us all," Mr. McClellan said.

One possible danger not listed in the book, however, is the book itself: today in Washington a copy of the book fell from a third-story apartment window, injuring three.

INSTRUMENT OF TERROR: A new government report lists baby grand pianos as potential weapons of mass destruction.

TALIBAN SHUTS DOWN REGIME; WILL FOCUS INSTEAD ON WEBSITE

Fall of Kabul, Weak Advertising Market Blamed

The Taliban, once the high-flying darling of the repressive regime sector, shut down its government today, but said that it would continue to exist on the Internet as "a website that delivers the total Taliban experience."

The site, Taliboom.com, will be operated by a skeleton staff and will offer a wide variety of repressive chat rooms and bulletin boards.

Taliban leader Mullah Omar announced the news of the shutdown to his staff at Taliban headquarters in Kandahar.

"For those of you who have been with us for the last five years, you know it's been an awesome ride," he told the assembled group, many of whom wore baseball caps embroidered with the Taliban slogan: "Have You Talibanned Something Today?"

For many Taliban in attendance, the news of the shutdown came almost as a relief.

"The rumor mill around this place has been working overtime," said one junior Taliban project manager. "I kind of knew something was up when I saw that this Northern Alliance guy had parked his Saturn in my space."

It was a very different story when the Taliban started up, in 1996, with a launch party that was the envy of repressive regimes worldwide.

But five years and many blown-up ancient statues later, the long-promised "synergy" of the

The Taliban remains committed to maintaining its popular website, Mullah Omar announced.

regime still remained elusive—and patience finally gave out.

"At the end of the day, our regime was grimmer, bleaker, and more repressive than we'd ever dreamed it could be—but it just wasn't profitable," Omar conceded.

The recent fall of Kabul, as well as the current weak advertising market, contributed to the Taliban's decision to close up shop.

"It's a different world now," Omar said. "The landscape has cratered—literally."

In addition to its government, the Taliban will close down its five-month-old lifestyles magazine, *Teen Taliban*, which many in the magazine industry considered to be ill conceived.

"We all worked real hard on *Teen Taliban*, but you can't make a turkey fly," Omar said.

ANN COULTER SPONTANEOUSLY COMBUSTS

Pundit Keeps Talking While Fully Ablaze

Conservative pundit Ann Coulter sponta-neously combusted today during an appearance on the Fox News Channel, sources at the cable network confirmed.

According to those who witnessed the bizarre incident, Ms. Coulter was in the middle of an extended rant about liberal comedian Al Franken when her face became beet-red and smoke began to shoot out of both of her ears.

Then, almost without warning, Ms. Coulter appeared to burst into flames, sources said.

The New York Fire Department immediately rushed to the scene to extinguish Ms. Coulter, who continued to talk even while fully ablaze.

"We were dousing her with three fire hoses, but she just kept on yapping," said Hal Reuss, a fireman who helped put out Ms. Coulter. "It was freaky."

Meanwhile, outside the Fox News Channel's New York headquarters, thousands of publicity-starved authors congregated, begging Fox to sue them.

Since news of Fox's lawsuit against come-dian Franken promptly sent his new book to the top of the bestseller lists, a lawsuit from Fox is now widely regarded in the publishing industry as the most coveted seal of approval, even sur-passing inclusion in Oprah's Book Club.

One of the authors gathered outside Fox was Stanley Dixon, an author of several poorly sell-ing works of literary fiction who is so eager to be sued by Fox that he has had his name legally changed to "Fox Newschannel."

Mr. Newschannel said that his latest novel, a coming-of-age story set in rural Indiana entitled *A Sudden Fall*, would now be retitled *The Fox News Channel Can Bite Me*.

Conservative pundit Ann Coulter appeared at a benefit in New York City one day before she sponta-neously burst into flames.

KIM'S BLOG

I've never told anybody this before, but back in the days before I acquired nuclear weapons technology from Pakistan, I seriously considered acquiring Ann Coulter.

I'd seen Ms. Coulter on TV, and she was always in a bad mood, screaming at somebody and making the veins in her forehead bulge out, and I was like, Dude! This is a weapon of mass destruction if ever there was one.

My plan was simple: add Ann Coulter to my burgeoning weapons arsenal, and if the U.S. refused to do my bidding, I'd fire Ann Coulter at them.

I even could picture a split-screen on TV: Ann Coulter on a launch pad, and me counting down, ten, nine, eight . . . *tell* me that would not rule!!

Like most simple plans, though, this one got complicated real fast. I opened negotiations with Ann Coulter's agent, and we started hammering out the broad strokes of a deal. I can honestly say that I have never offered to pay as much money for a weapons system as I was willing to cough up for Ann Coulter.

Ultimately, the deal broke down because she refused to move to Pyongyang. She said her "life" was in New York. Whatever! But every now and then I have this recurring dream where I'm blowing up the world with Ann Coulter. I still think it could happen someday.

PHILIP MORRIS CHANGES NAME TO ALTRIA; CHANGES NAME OF CIGARETTES TO "HEALTH STIX"

Boldest Rebranding Effort Ever, Experts Say

When tobacco giant Philip Morris changed its corporate name to "Altria" yesterday, it apparently was just getting started.

Officials from the newly renamed company announced today that their primary product, cigarettes, will now be known as "Health Stix."

"We want to assure our customers that, even though the name has changed, the product remains the same," said company spokesman Dirk Slive, who will now be known as Sandy Nice.

"And we hope that they will continue to smoke two or three packs of Health Stix each and every day," Mr. Nice added.

"Remember—they're good for you," Mr. Nice said, adding that Altria had recently changed the word "bad" to "good."

Company officials were asked if all of this renaming was intended to confuse the consumer.

"Hardly," Mr. Nice said. "We're doing it out of altruism—remember, we're not called Altria for nothing."

In a related decision, Altria has renamed tar and nicotine "sugar and spice," and will call hideously discolored brown teeth "chick magnets."

Altria believes that cigarettes will soar to new levels of popularity under their new name, "Health Stix."

In addition, desperate, hacking, phlegmy coughs will now be known as "breathing."

At press time, Altria officials were still mulling new names for death. While no decision has been reached as of yet, sources say that Altria executives were leaning heavily toward "Happy Nappy Time."

BILL BENNETT LOSES WIFE IN POKER GAME

Irate Spouse Demands He Win Her Back "This Instant"

Gambling woes have taken their toll on former Education Secretary William Bennett once again as Mr. Bennett revealed today that he lost his wife in a high-stakes poker game Saturday night.

"While I regret putting my wife on the table, I felt that my hand was really strong and there was no way I'd lose her," the *Book of Virtues* author said at a Washington press conference. "I was totally flabbergasted when Jim Baker countered with a royal flush."

A spokesman for former Secretary of State James A. Baker III confirmed that he had in fact won Mrs. Bennett in the Saturday night card game but refused to elaborate any further.

But in a statement released later today, Mrs. William Bennett excoriated her husband for putting her in the kitty of the poker game without her permission and demanded that he win her back "this instant."

Cornered by reporters outside his home, where he was arranging furniture and other personal items for an upcoming yard sale, Mr. Bennett said he had given up gambling for good and therefore had "no intention" of trying to win back his wife.

"Trying to win back Elayne at the poker table would be gambling, and I've learned that gambling is bad," he said. "I hope Elayne understands my position."

President Bush, who had been tight-lipped about the Bennett affair, later offered these words of support for the embattled Republican: "I'm glad Bill Bennett stopped gambling before he lost his shirt, because no one wants to see Bill Bennett without his shirt."

SOME 'SPLAINING TO DO: Former Education Secretary Bill Bennett reportedly angered his wife after losing her in a high-stakes poker game.

SADDAM DENIES PURSUING "NUCULAR" WEAPONS

No Evidence of Nucular Program in Iraq, Strongman Says

Responding to last night's State of the Union address in which President George W. Bush repeatedly accused him of attempting to acquire "nucular" weapons, President Saddam Hussein of Iraq today categorically denied having a "nucular" weapons program of any kind.

"Iraq does not now nor has it ever had a 'nucular' weapons program," Saddam said in a terse official statement. "Nor does it have any idea what a 'nucular' weapon is."

At the White House, Press Secretary Ari Fleischer accused Saddam of using Mr. Bush's pronunciation of "nucular" to distract attention from Iraq's persistent refusal to disarm.

"I think the international community knows that when the President says 'nucular' he means 'nuclear,'" Mr. Fleischer said. "We challenge Saddam to prove that he does not have any of the weapons that President Bush may have mispronounced last night."

Mr. Bush's State of the Union address drew support from an unlikely quarter today, as Nobel Peace Prize–winner Jimmy Carter announced that he "completely agreed" with the President's pronunciation of the word "nucular."

"Back when I was President, I often gave speeches about nucular energy, and everybody

YOU SAY "NUCULAR": The White House believes Saddam Hussein is using the President's pronunciation of "nucular" to avoid revealing a massive weapons cache.

always knew what I was talking about," Mr. Carter said. "I think people should back off."

In other international pronunciation news, Prime Minister Tony Blair of Britain split with President Bush today over his pronunciation of the words "tomato" and "banana."

While Mr. Blair indicated that he and Mr. Bush had "a serious difference of opinion" about how "tomato" and "banana" were pronounced, he said it would in no way affect Britain's support of a U.S.-led attack on Iraq.

IT'S SPLITSVILLE FOR ANGELINA JOLIE AND HER BREASTS

Actress, Chest Part Company, Citing "Creative Differences"

In a move that surprised many in Hollywood in the wake of the smash summer block-buster *Tomb Raider*, Angelina Jolie and her breasts announced today that they would no longer work together, citing "creative differences" as the reason for their split.

While official spokesmen for Ms. Jolie and her breasts publicly described the split as "amicable," insiders indicated that it was in fact a bitter parting, the inevitable result of rivalries growing out of the *Tomb Raider* success.

"It bothered Angelina that her breasts got better reviews than she did, but she was willing to swallow her pride and continue working with them," said Skip Winston, a longtime Hollywood press agent. "This thing was a hundred percent the breasts' decision."

Others in the industry agreed with Winston's assessment. "There was a feeling that people were hiring Angelina just as a way of getting to work with her breasts," said talent agent Herb Schlantz. "From what I've heard, the breasts were getting tired of carrying her."

Now that the split is official, there has been no word about what the breasts' next project will be, but there are already signs that there is "trouble in paradise," as one insider put it.

"Apparently, the left breast is slightly larger than the right breast," the insider said, "and the left breast feels that should be reflected in the billing."

As of press time, there was no confirmation of the rumors that the breasts were planning a split-up of their own in order to pursue solo careers.

Ms. Jolie's breasts could not be reached for comment.

Ms. Jolie and her breasts, in happier times.

WEALTHIEST .00001 PERCENT PRAISE BUSH ECONOMIC PACKAGE

At Annual Gathering in Geneva, 29 Richest Americans Give Plan Big Thumbs-Up

President Bush's newly unveiled economic stimulus package drew raves today from the wealthiest .00001 percent of Americans, who pronounced the plan "a total home run."

"When we first heard about the plan, we were like, this is too good to be true," said multibillionaire Thurston Howell IV, a spokesman for the richest .00001 percent. "But when our butlers read the plan aloud to us during the cocktail hour, we were incredibly stoked."

The twenty-nine plutocrats who make up the nation's wealthiest .00001 percent were at their

The super-rich believe that the Bush tax package could transform them into the super-duper-rich.

annual meeting at Mr. Howell's villa in Geneva, Switzerland, when news of the President's plan was first released.

"Bill Gates and Warren Buffett were the first to hear about it, and then the news just kind of trickled down, if I may use a favorite phrase of ours," Mr. Howell said.

Mr. Howell added that the elimination of all Federal taxes on dividends would provide much-needed relief to him and the other twenty-eight wealthiest Americans, who have been "struggling to make ends meet on our dividends alone."

"The President deserves credit for recognizing what the wealthiest .00001 percent have known for years," Mr. Howell said. "It's well-nigh impossible to maintain a dozen households around the world, stable after stable of racehorses and a fleet of private jets if your dividends are being taxed."

Mr. Howell differed with the President only in one minor detail—the theory that the new round of tax cuts would stimulate spending by the wealthiest Americans.

"Anyone who thinks we're going to spend more just doesn't know how the wealthiest .00001 percent thinks," Howell said. "We're stingy fucks."

NEW TAPE MAY MEAN AL GORE IS ALIVE

Intelligence Analysts Studying Chilling Today Show Appearance

A videotape purporting to show former Vice President Al Gore appearing on NBC's *Today* show with Katie Couric to promote a new book is the strongest evidence to date that Mr. Gore may be alive, intelligence sources said today.

While the former Democratic standard-bearer had been virtually invisible since the 2000 election, leading many to believe that he had disappeared for good, the *Today* show tape offered chilling proof that he may in fact be alive and could be threatening to run for President again.

U.S. intelligence analysts were said to be closely examining the tape to determine if the person sitting on Ms. Couric's couch is in fact Mr. Gore, but were withholding a final verdict until further analysis could be performed.

"The person on the tape could very well be Al Gore," said a source familiar with the videotape. "On the other hand, it could also be a full-sized wooden puppet painted to resemble Al Gore."

The source said that the process of authenticating the tape was made more difficult by the fact that it is "almost impossible" to tell the difference between Mr. Gore and a full-sized wooden puppet, the chief difference being that

A chilling new tape features a man who looks much like former Vice President Al Gore (right), suggesting that Mr. Gore may be alive, as some have feared.

a wooden puppet is "slightly more animated."

Intelligence analysts are comparing the *Today* show tape to tapes of Mr. Gore's 2000 debates to determine if in fact Mr. Gore is alive, as some Democratic strategists fear he may be.

"What's tricky about this is that after looking at the tapes of the debates, it's not clear that Al Gore was alive back in 2000, either," the source said.

KIM'S BLOG

We've got a little joke around the office in Pyongyang. When somebody does something really loser-y, instead of going "Loser!" we'll go "Al Gore!" Like most jokes, this one has the element of truth, which is why it's so funny.

I mean, really, how do you get more votes than the other guy and still wind up not getting elected? To me, this is a pretty good reason for not having any elections at all (like I needed a reason!!).

Every now and then, though, my political advisors tell me that running for election in North Korea would be a good thing, politically. I mean, I know everybody loves me and all, but it would be awesome to have the numbers to prove it. The only thing that's stopped me so far has been that one nagging question: "What if I wind up like Al Gore, and get the most votes, but still lose?"

That's when I had a brainstorm: if I ever run for President of North Korea, I'll run against Al Gore! I don't think it's physically possible to lose an election to Al Gore—it defies all the laws of the universe.

I guess there's always a remote chance that Al Gore would beat me somehow, but if he did, I'd just explode a nuclear bomb on his head. I'm all for experimenting with democracy, but I'm not nuts.

MICROSOFT BUYS MASSACHUSETTS

State to be Renamed "Microchusetts"

Software giant Microsoft bought the entire Commonwealth of Massachusetts today, thus removing the last remaining obstacle to its antitrust settlement with the U.S. Justice Department.

In a statement released today at Microsoft headquarters in Redmond, Washington, company cofounders William Gates and Steven Ballmer confirmed that they had purchased Massachusetts "lock, stock and barrel" for $17.2 billion, which is believed to be the state's breakup value.

"We are looking forward to integrating Massachusetts into our operations and making this historic state a vibrant part of the Microsoft family," the statement read, adding that the state will now be known as "Microchusetts."

In Massachusetts, Microsoft is purchasing a state with a storied past, beginning with its role as one of the original thirteen colonies of what was eventually to become the United States of America.

But it is also buying the only state that had appealed the Justice Department's landmark antitrust settlement with Microsoft, an appeal that is likely to be dropped now.

Former Massachusetts Attorney General Tom Reilly, who was personally given his walking papers by Mr. Ballmer late Saturday night, cautioned that Microsoft's acquisition of Massachusetts "doesn't pass the smell test."

But while some legal experts believe that the acquisition of a major U.S. state may create new antitrust woes for the software giant, Gates and Ballmer hope to appease Justice Department lawyers by spinning off the Boston Red Sox, a franchise in which the Microsoft cofounders are said to have "no interest" in retaining.

Across the state today, citizens seemed to be taking Massachusetts' evolution from a U.S. state to a division of Microsoft in stride.

"We'll probably have better dental," one Massachusetts resident said.

Microsoft founder Bill Gates tells shareholders that the company has completed its controversial acquisition of the Commonwealth of Massachusetts.

CHENEY, BRIEFLY ASSUMING BUSH'S DUTIES, SAYS HE ENJOYED THE DOWNTIME

President's Colon Procedure Offered Welcome Break from Grueling Vice Presidential Schedule

Vice President Dick Cheney, having briefly assumed President Bush's duties while the President underwent a routine colon procedure on Saturday, told reporters today that he "enjoyed the downtime immensely."

The two hours and fifteen minutes spent doing Bush's job were "incredibly relaxing," Mr. Cheney said, adding that they were a welcome relief from his exacting vice presidential schedule.

Invoking the Twenty-fifth Amendment to the Constitution Saturday morning, Mr. Bush transferred to Mr. Cheney all of his presidential responsibilities, which meant that Mr. Cheney spent Saturday jogging, going to the gym, and hitting a ball for Mr. Bush's dog to retrieve.

In addition, Mr. Cheney called the nations of East Timor and Luxembourg "evil," stumbling briefly over the pronunciation of Luxembourg.

Finally, as Mr. Bush's colon procedure was winding down, Mr. Cheney made some remarks about the Japanese economy, mistakenly using the word "devaluation" instead of "deflation," sending the Nikkei stock market into a tailspin.

All in all, Mr. Cheney said he emerged from his brief tenure as President rested and refreshed, ready to plunge back into his demanding vice presidential workload.

As for the President, Mr. Bush's doctors pronounced his procedure a success, but said that they were having difficulty determining whether or not the President's anesthesia had fully worn off.

Mr. Bush's doctors indicated that when they asked the President the standard postoperative questions—such as "What is the capital of the United States?"—Mr. Bush got only two out of five correct.

"Before the operation, he got three out of five right," one doctor said.

Mr. Cheney called his time assuming the President's duties "a much-needed rest."

MAN, 37, SEES *MONA LISA SMILE*

Suffered No Lasting Damage, Medical Expert Says

An Indiana man who had intended to see the Russell Crowe adventure film *Master and Commander* last Saturday night accidentally bought a ticket to the Julia Roberts chick-flick *Mona Lisa Smile* instead and watched the movie until its conclusion, sources close to the man revealed today.

Brian Hogan, 37, of Gary, Indiana, is believed to be the only man in America who has actually sat through the *Mona Lisa* film in its entirety.

Friends of Mr. Hogan said that being subjected to the soapy tearjerker was "a scarring experience" for the tool-and-die sales rep, who had been looking forward to celebrating his birthday Saturday night by watching a movie with a lot of things blowing up in it.

There is little in the medical literature documenting the effects of a three-hanky film on a man's health, says Dr. Harold Crone of the University of Minnesota Medical School.

"There is only one famous case, that of a man who accidentally wandered into a showing of the Barbra Streisand film *The Way We Were*, in 1973," says Dr. Crone. "In that case, there was no lasting medical damage, and the man went on to perform a very successful cabaret act."

Dr. Crone said that the worst-case scenario for Mr. Hogan would be that his body might undergo "slight changes," as if he had accidentally ingested a small amount of female hormones.

At press time, Mr. Hogan was refusing to answer reporters' questions, saying only that he was "hurt and upset" that they had forgotten his birthday.

Exposure to Julia Roberts films such as *Mona Lisa Smile* may have no lasting hormonal effects on men, medical experts say.

FBI ORDERS "WHILE-YOU-WERE-OUT" MESSAGE PADS

Trip to OfficeMax Crucial to Agency's Overhaul, Mueller Says

In what its director described as a "crucial" first step to upgrade the Federal Bureau of Investigation's intelligence-gathering capabilities, the FBI paid a visit to an OfficeMax superstore today and bought "a substantial number" of While-You-Were-Out message pads.

The agency, which has never had access to such message pads in the past, believes that the introduction of the While-You-Were-Out pads will dramatically improve the relaying of phone messages at FBI headquarters and in field offices across the country.

FBI Director Robert Mueller, speaking at a press conference in Washington, D.C, said that the FBI had also purchased "these little yellow reminder thingies with stick-um stuff on the back so you can post them on your desk and whatnot."

Mueller added that the FBI was "intrigued" by a machine they saw at OfficeMax that could record phone messages and store them while an FBI employee was away from his or her desk.

"Once the phone messages are played back, they could theoretically be written down on the While-You-Were-Out pads," Mueller said.

While Mueller pronounced the trip to Office-Max "a resounding success," FBI whistleblower Colleen Rowley revealed today that she had urged the agency to invest in While-You-Were-Out pads months ago—but no one listened.

"I then tried to write a memo about it, but there were no pens or paper anywhere in the office," Rowley complained. "This visit to Office-Max, I'm afraid, is too little too late."

For his part, Mueller said he welcomed Rowley's latest round of criticism.

"I'm always delighted to have Colleen Rowley rip me a new one," Mueller said.

The FBI's visit to OfficeMax to purchase While-You-Were-Out message pads represents a major ramping up in the war on terror, FBI officials say.

SOTHEBY'S AUCTIONS RARE HOME MOVIES OF BOB CRANE NOT HAVING SEX

Startling Footage of Fully Clothed Hogan Fetches Record Bid

In London today, leading auction house Sotheby's auctioned a reel of rare, recently discovered home movies of *Hogan's Heroes* actor Bob Crane not having sex.

The extaordinary footage of a fully clothed Crane engaged in such nonsexual activities as reading the newspaper and washing his car fetched a winning bid of $1.825 million, exceeding even Sotheby's most optimistic expectations.

"Given that these are, to our knowledge, the only home movies of Mr. Crane not having sex, the high price is justified," said Clive Widdington, a spokesman for the auction house.

The rare footage, discovered in the attic of a home in El Paso, Texas, where Mr. Crane had appeared in dinner theater in the seventies, at first appeared to be a hoax.

"When I first saw the videos, I said to myself that this could not possibly be Bob Crane," said Dr. Bernard Fulton of the University of Minnesota. "For one thing, he had his pants on."

But Dr. Fulton, who teaches a graduate course in the home movies of Bob Crane and ultimately authenticated the sex-free Crane footage, warned that the movies "should not

For decades, collectors have been searching for rare home videos of actor Bob Crane not having sex, Sotheby's confirmed.

force us to call into question all of our previous thinking about Bob Crane."

"Even though he is not having sex in these movies, it's safe to say that he's thinking about having sex," Dr. Fulton said.

The winning bid for the footage of Bob Crane not having sex established a new record for a celebrity home movie auctioned by Sotheby's, topping the $1.675 million paid for a 1997 home movie of actress Pamela Anderson not having sex.

BUSH ACCUSES IRAQ OF HIDING WEAPONS IN NORTH KOREA

Calls North Koreans Dupes of Saddam's Latest Scam

In a bombshell with serious ramifications for U.S. foreign policy, President Bush today accused Iraqi strongman Saddam Hussein of hiding nuclear weapons in North Korea.

While the President offered no hard evidence to back up his startling claim, he insisted that the so-called secret North Korean nuclear weapons program was actually a secret Iraqi nuclear weapons program.

He went on to quote intelligence reports suggesting that Saddam Hussein had sent the weapons to North Korea in big wooden crates stamped with the logo of Harry & David's, a popular food-by-mail gift service, to avoid interdiction en route.

"This may be the evilest thing this doer of evil has ever done," Mr. Bush said.

Mr. Bush's stunning announcement may have been meant to deflect criticism of the administration's policy of being mean to Iraq but not quite so mean to North Korea.

But North Korea complicated that effort somewhat by announcing later in the day that the weapons were in fact their own and did not come from Iraq, adding that Saddam Hussein did not even have North Korea's mailing address or home phone number.

For his part, the President quickly dismissed North Korea's denials, calling the North Koreans "dupes" of Saddam's evil plan to sneak nuclear weapons into their country.

"The fact that Saddam has snuck evil weapons into North Korea and has somehow convinced the North Koreans that they made them themselves just goes to show you how dangerous Iraq is and how not-dangerous North Korea is," the President said.

North Korean soldiers stand guard near a supersecret hiding place where Iraqi dictator Saddam Hussein is believed to have hidden weapons of mass destruction.

KIM'S BLOG

During the months leading up to the war with Iraq, Bush and Colin Powell and Condoleezza Rice and Donald Rumsfeld kept going on TV talking about how dangerous Saddam Hussein was, and I was like, What am I, chopped liver?

You've got to understand—I've spent half my life trying to prove how evil I am. My reputation is totally based on that. If people don't think I'm evil, what do I have to show for all of those reprocessed spent fuel rods? Jack shit, that's what.

So here comes Saddam Hussein, who's basically just been sitting in Baghdad getting fat and with those two loser sons of his, *pretending* like he's got all of this awesome bio-shit (Dr. Germ, Mrs. Anthrax—fuck, those people sounded like characters out of *Clue*) and suddenly he's the most evil guy in the world? Excuse me, but that sucks.

Then I turned on the TV on Halloween and there were American kids trick-or-treating as Saddam Hussein. Not a single Kim Jong Il mask in the bunch. Hellooo! Earth to America! Evil guy over here! Restarting nuclear reactors!

I don't want to make it look like Saddam and I have a whole Freddy vs. Jason thing going, but come on! After a while, it's pretty hard to take. I'm cranking out seven fucking nuclear weapons a day—give me my props already.

DENNIS MILLER TAKES OBSCURE, HARD-TO-UNDERSTAND PARTING SHOT AT ABC

Fired Monday Night Football *Comic's Rant Full of Puzzling Cultural References*

Comedian Dennis Miller, fired from ABC's *Monday Night Football* last week, lashed out at ABC Sports today in a blistering tirade packed with obscure literary and pop cultural references that may take his former bosses years to decipher.

"Hey, you guys pulled a Pete Best on me," Miller told the executives at ABC Sports. "Well, you don't need to show me the exit. Who am I, Jean-Paul Sartre?"

The ABC executives begged Miller to slow down so that they could look up some of the items contained in the often-baffling comedian's trademark "rant," but Miller, seemingly undeterred, soldiered on in the same arcane vein.

"When I heard you were replacing me with Madden, I was like, isn't that the guy who played Reuben Kincaid on *The Partridge Family?*" Miller said, in an apparent reference to football announcer John Madden and former TV actor Dave Madden.

It is believed that only three or four people in North America, excluding Miller himself, are sufficiently aware of both Maddens in order to

A spokesman for ABC said the network was confused by many of the obscure cultural references in a statement released by comedian Dennis Miller.

understand, and therefore enjoy, Miller's confusing remark.

Skewering announcer Madden's use of the "telestrator" to diagram football plays, Miller said, "That guy makes more points than Georges Seurat on the Island of the Grande Jatte. Calling Stephen Sondheim!"

O'NEILL FIRED OVER "IT'S THE ECONOMY, STUPID" REMARK

"Don't Call Me Stupid," Bush Shot Back

A clearer picture of the events leading up to Treasury Secretary Paul H. O'Neill's forced resignation was revealed today, as White House aides said that Mr. O'Neill was undone by unintentionally calling the President "stupid" in a meeting last week.

The heated exchange occurred at the White House late Thursday night, aides said, when Mr. O'Neill urged the President to focus more on the economy, telling Mr. Bush, "Remember, it's the economy, stupid."

Mr. Bush's face reportedly reddened with rage after Mr. O'Neill made his remark.

"I know it's the economy," the President replied, "and don't call me 'stupid.'"

Mr. O'Neill quickly defended his "it's the economy, stupid" remark as a figure of speech, but the President "would have none of it," aides said.

"I know when someone's called me stupid, and you just called me stupid," Mr. Bush said. "Well if I'm stupid, you're a dickwad. How do you like them apples?"

Mr. O'Neill, realizing that he had walked into a rhetorical minefield, quickly attempted to mend fences with the President.

"When I said 'it's the economy, stupid,' I just meant that the economy is something you should focus more on," Mr. O'Neill said.

"Who are you calling a moron?" a furious Mr. Bush demanded, leaping from his chair.

"It's 'whom,'" corrected Lawrence B. Lindsey, director of the National Economic Council, who was also present at the meeting.

Moments after Mr. Lindsey's "whom" remark, the President called him a "smart-ass" and abruptly demanded his resignation as well.

"If there's one thing the President hates more than being called stupid, it's being corrected on that whole who-whom thing," one aide said.

"DON'T CALL ME STUPID": An unfortunate turn of phrase may have ended Paul O'Neill's troubled tenure as Treasury Secretary.

CHENEY'S BRIEF APPEARANCE, RETURN TO SECURE LOCATION MAY MEAN SIX MORE WEEKS OF WINTER

White House Downplays Veep's Influence Over Seasons

Vice President Dick Cheney emerged from his secure, undisclosed location to make the rounds of the morning news programs this Sunday, but then immediately returned to his hiding place—indicating that America may be in for six more weeks of winter, according to experts.

While appearing with Tim Russert on NBC's *Meet the Press*, observers say, the Vice President seemed distracted, looking over his shoulder repeatedly as if trying to see his own shadow.

Vice President Dick Cheney (left) might have seen his shadow while appearing on NBC's *Meet the Press* with Tim Russert.

A review of the broadcast indicates that Vice President Cheney, in fact, appeared to locate his shadow toward the end of the program.

He then abruptly concluded the interview, canceled an appearance with CNN's Wolf Blitzer and returned to his secure, undisclosed location, which is believed to be underground.

Experts were divided as to the impact of Mr. Cheney's brief appearance and sudden disappearance upon the duration of the current winter season.

"You can read anything you want into Cheney seeing his own shadow and going back underground," said Dr. Evan Cornwall of the University of Minnesota. "Yes, it may mean six more weeks of winter, but it may just mean that he's trying to stay as far away from the Enron mess as possible."

At the White House, spokesman Scott McClellan attempted to downplay the increasingly widespread impression that Vice President Cheney can influence the seasons.

"It's absurd to suggest that the Vice President can control the weather," Mr. McClellan told reporters. "He's got his hands full controlling the world."

U.N. TO BEGIN WEAPONS INSPECTIONS SOMETIME BETWEEN 8 AND 12 THIS MORNING; ASKS IRAQ IF SOMEONE WILL BE HOME

Saddam Demands "More Exact Time"

U.N. weapons inspectors have informed Iraq that they will be arriving to look for weapons of mass destruction sometime between 8 A.M. and 12 noon today and have asked if someone will be home to let them in.

In a potential roadblock to the weapons inspection process, however, Iraqi strongman Saddam Hussein has demanded that the inspectors give "a more exact time" when he can expect them to arrive.

In a sharply worded statement, the Iraqi leader said he was "too busy oppressing my people and purging members of my own family to spend the entire morning waiting for the inspectors to show up."

Saddam added that the last time U.N. inspectors came to look for weapons of mass destruction in his country, "they said they'd come in the morning, and I waited until two in the afternoon before they finally showed up. It was totally bogus."

The weapons inspectors defended their tardiness, however, saying that Iraq had not been first on the schedule for that day and that weapons in-

The U.N. refused to give Saddam Hussein a more exact time for its weapons inspections visit this week.

spections in other rogue nations had "run late."

In addition, the U.N. encouraged Saddam o avail himself of the toll-free automated weapons inspection hotline that the world body has set up especially for him and other evil despots.

A caller to the toll-free number reaches a recorded voice indicating the following prompts: "Press 1 if you are hiding chemical weapons; press 2 if you are hiding biological weapons; press 3 if you are hoping to acquire fissionable nuclear material in the next six to twelve months."

INCREASINGLY, ALIENS ARE CREATING HALF-ASSED CROP CIRCLES

Farmers Bemoan Lazy Space Creatures' Shoddy Workmanship

In M. Night Shyamalan's hit movie *Signs*, Mel Gibson sees a crop circle suddenly appear in the cornfield behind his shingled farmhouse, igniting a supernatural mystery.

But to most American farmers, crop circles are becoming a major annoyance, as lazy, careless aliens increasingly leave their cornfields without completing an attractive design—making the farmers wish the little green slackers had never landed in the first place.

"Some might call what I've got in my cornfield back there a crop circle," says Bud Fortenson, a farmer in eastern Idaho. "I call it a big old mess."

Aliens landed in Mr. Fortenson's cornfield last June and began creating what the farmer thought would be a "really neat" crop circle, Mr. Fortenson said.

But after two weeks of working on the crop circle, the aliens got bored with their work, complained that their backs hurt, and abruptly departed—leaving Mr. Fortenson's cornfield severely mutilated, a far cry from a completed crop circle.

"It looks like a guy just got drunk and went nuts with a John Deere out there," Mr. Forten-

Farmers have been voicing annoyance at what they claim is "increasingly shoddy workmanship" in alien crop circles.

son said. "If that's a crop circle, then I'm Liza Minnelli."

Half-assed crop circles are increasingly becoming a serious nuisance in rural America, says Dr. Phyllis DeVore, who studies half-assed alien phenomena at the University of Minnesota.

"Just because they're intelligent, that doesn't mean aliens are intrinsically hardworking or conscientious," Dr. DeVore says. "It's just as likely that they're capable of doing a half-assed, slipshod job."

Dr. DeVore said that many half-assed phenomena in the world today might actually have been the work of lazy aliens, including the *Legally Blonde* sequel and Justin Timberlake's entire recording career.

PAPER THAT ENRON STOCK IS PRINTED ON IS WORTHLESS, TOO, PAPER EXPERTS SAY

Stock Certificates Dissolve, Spontaneously Combust on Contact, Tests Show

For weeks, Enron shareholders have been hearing that their stock isn't worth the paper it's printed on. Now comes word that the paper it's printed on is worthless, too.

Those are the findings of Dr. Franklin Glaser of the National Paper-Testing Institute in Bethesda, Maryland, who says that Enron stock certificates are printed on paper that is "far below acceptable standards for negotiable securities" and that has "no value" for such other purposes as gift-wrap or place mats.

"People stuck with Enron stock in their 401k accounts may have comforted themselves with the thought that they could use it to make festive paper hats," Dr. Glaser said. "Unfortunately, if they try to fold an Enron stock certificate, it will dissolve into dust."

Not only are Enron stock certificates worthless, they may actually be dangerous, Dr. Glaser said.

"In lab tests, our team found that Enron stock certificates, on occasion, spontaneously combust or explode when touched," Dr. Glaser said. "This makes them highly unsuitable for most uses in the home or office."

It is extremely unusual, Dr. Glaser said, for stock certificates to be printed on paper stock that dissolves, burns up, or explodes when handled, but his team has a theory to explain the phenomenon.

The paper experts believe that Enron stock was mistakenly printed on a special self-destructing paper stock intended for Enron spreadsheets, accounting statements and transcripts of meetings with Vice President Richard Cheney.

The paper that Enron stock certificates are printed on is of a significantly lower quality than other stock certificates, paper experts say.

BUSH WINS NOBEL WAR PRIZE

Saddam Miffed at Oslo Snub

The Norwegian Nobel Committee honored President George W. Bush today by bestowing upon him the first-ever Nobel War Prize.

In Oslo, Nobel Committee Chairman Gunnar Berge said that Mr. Bush was chosen for the award because "above all, in his words and deeds, President Bush has stood for the resolution of conflicts between nations and peoples through the use of massive and overwhelming force."

At the White House, President Bush said that he was surprised to have received the Nobel War Prize and that he was "deeply honored and touched."

He added that it would have been impossible to win the award without the help of Senate Majority Leader Tom Daschle, whom the President thanked for "his tireless efforts to do absolutely nothing to hinder me."

But even as the Oslo committee announced the first-ever prize, there was a firestorm of controversy in international circles, with some critics charging that President Bush was insufficiently bellicose to win the Nobel War Prize.

In particular, Iraqi strongman Saddam Hussein expressed the view that he and not the President should have walked off with the coveted Norwegian accolade.

"I've been busting my hump to win the Nobel War Prize for the better part of twenty years, and he just scoops it up at the last minute?" a visibly miffed Saddam said to reporters in Baghdad. "Excuse me, but the whole thing reeks of politics."

For his part, President Bush brushed off Saddam's comments as "sour grapes," and said he would use the $1 million award to break ground on the Bush Center for Preemptive Armed Conflict in Houston, Texas.

President Bush told reporters that he was "gratified and humbled" by the news that he had won the coveted Nobel War Prize.

CIA USING AMERICAN CEOS TO INFILTRATE AL-QAEDA

Agency Expects Terror Group to Collapse Within Weeks

Former Vivendi Universal chief Jean-Marie Messier (pictured) may have played a pivotal role in the CIA's plan to drive al-Qaeda into bankruptcy.

The CIA acknowledged today that it has been employing disgraced CEOs of *Fortune* 500 companies to infiltrate al-Qaeda and that it expects the international terror group to collapse within weeks.

"We believe that the forces of evil have finally met their match," a CIA spokesman said.

While the CIA would not identify which corporate sleazebags had been used in the highly sensitive operation, intelligence sources believe they were plucked from the ranks of Tyco, Enron, Adelphia, WorldCom, Sotheby's and over ninety other recently disgraced companies.

The unidentified CEOs have reportedly been so successful in cooking al-Qaeda's books that the once-flush terror network is now $30 billion in debt and may have to sell its long-profitable terror training camps at fire-sale prices.

In addition to the undercover CEO operation, the CIA is reportedly considering employing recently departed Vivendi Universal chief Jean-Marie Messier in a mission to force the terror group into several highly leveraged, ill-advised media acquisitions.

According to the rumors, Monsieur Messier would steer the terror group's resources toward idiotic Internet and telecom ventures, as well as the purchase of a $17.5 million Park Avenue residence for Osama bin Laden.

The CIA poured cold water on those rumors, however, saying that it regarded Monsieur Messier as "a weapon of last resort."

"The use of Monsieur Messier would create so much devastation, it's really in the realm of the unthinkable," the spokesman said.

HOLLYWOOD GROUP PROTESTS WAR, LACK OF GOOD ROLES FOR WOMEN OVER FORTY

France, Germany, Russia Join in Call for Better Scripts

A group of unemployed Hollywood film actors has planned a march on Washington, D.C., for later today to protest the war with Iraq and the lack of good roles for women over forty, a spokesperson for the group said.

"The Bush administration is so focused on Saddam Hussein, they've completely lost sight of the crisis in women's film roles," said Gillian Hartnell, spokesperson for the Hollywood Coalition for Peace and Better Parts.

Money spent on the war in Iraq could be used to develop better scripts for aging actresses like Susan Sarandon and Meg Ryan, Hollywood protesters said.

"We may not know whether Saddam Hussein has weapons of mass destruction or not, but one thing we do know is that most of us have not gotten any film work in at least a decade," Ms. Hartnell added.

Ms. Hartnell said that many in her group were frustrated by the resources that were being poured into impending military action against Baghdad that could be used instead to fund "scripts showing women over forty being strong, sexy and vibrant."

"And instead of offering Turkey thirty billion dollars to base American troops there, we should be using that money to pay for more flattering eight-by-ten glossies of unemployed actresses," Ms. Hartnell said.

The foreign ministers of France, Germany and Russia plan to join the group's march in Washington today, with French Foreign Minister Dominique de Villepin excoriating the U.S.'s treatment of actresses over forty as "disgraceful."

"I just rented, how you say, *Scooby-Doo*," Monsieur de Villepin said. "Where were the women in that film? The screenwriters gave all the best lines to the dog. You Americans disgust me."

U2'S BONO PROPOSES SWEEPING SOCIAL SECURITY OVERHAUL

But Plan Faces Stiff Opposition from Aerosmith's Steven Tyler

I n a sign that he intends to step up his day-to-day involvement in the workings of the Federal government, Irish rocker Bono of the platinum-selling band U2 delivered a 1,062-page plan to Congress today to insure the Social Security program's solvency through fiscal year 2050.

But Bono gave a sneak preview one night earlier, interrupting a U2 concert at London's Wembley Stadium to explain his proposal.

"In 2000, the Social Security system took in five hundred sixty-eight billion dollars and paid out four hundred fifteen billion," Bono told the standing-room-only crowd in a forty-five-minute presentation complete with pie charts and bar graphs.

"But some privatization of the program will be necessary to insure its solvency when the so-called Baby Boom generation retires," said Bono, who coauthored the proposal with U2 guitarist The Edge.

While Bono's plan is garnering high marks on both sides of the aisle in Congress, it faces stiff opposition from one quarter: Aerosmith front man Steven Tyler, who excoriated Bono's proposal at an Aerosmith concert in Foxboro, Massachusetts.

"Bono's plan requires breaking into the So-

WITH OR WITHOUT YOU: U2 lead singer Bono (pictured) lashed out at Steven Tyler's proposed overhaul of Social Security.

cial Security lockbox by fiscal year 2012," said Tyler, interrupting a verse of Aerosmith's smash hit "Jaded" to talk about Social Security. "My plan doesn't go anywhere near the lockbox."

Tyler delivered his own 1,312-page Social Security proposal to Congress this morning, and while some in Washington welcomed the attention that the two rockers were bringing to the issue, others remained nonplussed.

"Quite frankly, I think we were all better off when these guys were just trashing hotel rooms and flipping over vans," said one member of the House Ways and Means Committee.

KIM'S BLOG

One thing people don't realize about Kim Jong Il is that I'm a mad crazy pop music nut. When I'm not threatening to blow up the world, you're likely to see me back at the house, grooving to some awesome tunes on my iPod. (I'm a mad crazy dancer, too, by the way.)

Because so few people know this musical side of me, I've never been asked to be a guest on one of those *Desert Island Disks* radio shows. You know what I'm talking about—where they ask you what records you'd bring with you on a deserted island. (Since I might wind up on a desert island after destroying the Korean Peninsula, this is far from an idle question!)

I guess my top five tunes would go something like this:

1. "Eve of Destruction" by Barry McGuire—I read somewhere that this was a protest song. Protesting what, I'd like to know? I put it on my party tape, and it rocks.

2. "Smoke on the Water" by Deep Purple—Every time this song comes on, I close my eyes and think of the Sea of Japan.

3. "Burning Down the House" by Talking Heads—When I sing it, I sing the word "South" instead of "House."

4. "Disco Inferno" by the Trammps—If I ruled the world, this would be the world's anthem. Well, it's only a matter of time, I guess.

5. "It's the End of the World As We Know It" by R.E.M.—And I feel fine!

BUSH: DEMOCRACY WILL COME TO IRAQ AND MAY EVENTUALLY REACH U.S.

President Offers Rosiest Postwar Scenario to Date

In a nationally televised speech tonight, President George W. Bush predicted that democracy would come to postwar Iraq and might eventually reach the U.S. as well.

"A new regime in Iraq would serve as a dramatic and inspiring example of freedom to other nations of the region," Mr. Bush said. "And who knows? If democracy works in Iraq, we might give it a try, too."

The President, under criticism for not laying out his vision for a postwar Iraq, said, "In a democratic Iraq, a President would be legitimately elected by a majority of the popular vote, not by mysterious electors or politically appointed robed justices."

Such an Iraqi President, Mr. Bush said, "would listen to all of the voices in his country, and not merely pander to extremists or corrupt moneyed interests."

In addition, the President said, "In a democratic Iraq, those who choose to voice their dissent by protesting will be recognized and listened to, not derided and ignored."

While President Bush stopped short of saying that an Iraqi-style democracy could take root in the U.S. in the near future, he added

Iraq could be a test case to determine whether democracy might eventually flourish in the U.S., Bush believes.

hopefully, "You never know—it could happen."

Immediately following his speech, White House Press Secretary Ari Fleischer tempered Mr. Bush's remarks somewhat, saying that the President "was speaking metaphorically" about the prospects for democracy in the United States.

"The President does in fact believe that democracy will come to the United States after the war is over," Mr. Fleischer said, "but not a moment sooner."

O.J. NO LONGER "100 PERCENT SURE" HE IS INNOCENT

Calls Johnnie Cochran's Recent Statements "Thought-Provoking"

Days after former O. J. Simpson defense attorney Johnnie Cochran admitted he is no longer 100 percent certain that his client was innocent, Mr. Simpson today said that his attorney had planted "fresh seeds of doubt" in his own mind.

"For years, I've been pretty sure that I did not murder my wife," Mr. Simpson said today at a golf course in Boca Raton, Florida, where he was taking a rare break from searching for the real killers of his wife. "But if Johnnie's not 100 percent sure, I'm like, hey, maybe I better take another look at this."

Mr. Simpson added that it would be "crazy" not to be swayed by Mr. Cochran's new statements, which he called "thought-provoking."

"Look, you're talking about a guy, Johnnie Cochran, who is a pretty smart guy," Mr. Simpson said. "If he said maybe I did it, then maybe I did it."

Mr. Cochran's doubts about Mr. Simpson's innocence may help resolve one lingering mystery for the former Heisman Trophy winner: why it has been so difficult for him to find his wife's real killers, whom he pledged to hunt down after his acquittal in 1995.

The former NFL star said that, in light of the new revelations, he may slow down his search,

Attorney Johnnie Cochran's comments have former NFL star O. J. Simpson (pictured) wondering if he might be guilty after all.

which he said has occupied almost every waking moment of his life for the past seven years.

"If it turns out that I'm actually the one who did it, then looking for the real killers would be a big old waste of time," Mr. Simpson said.

JOURNALIST EMBEDDED WITH FOX NEWS

Assigned to Cover "Fair and Balanced" Network for Duration of War

As part of an experimental new program initiated by the Defense Department, a journalist has been embedded with the FOX News Network, giving him unique access to the "fair and balanced" network for the duration of Operation Iraqi Freedom.

David Peterson, a reporter for the *Akron Beacon Journal*, will be the only journalist living, working and eating with Fox News staffers in the weeks to come.

Mr. Peterson said that although he felt very much "like an outsider" at the beginning of his stint with Fox News, he said that a mutual respect has grown between him and his hosts.

"I think at first it was weird for them to have a journalist around," Mr. Peterson said.

Mr. Peterson said that he does his best to stay out of the way of his Fox News comrades, adding, "They have their job to do and I have mine."

While the veteran journalist said he was excited about being embedded with Fox News, he admitted that his first days at the news channel had provided him with more than a few hair-raising moments.

"You can prepare all you want to be embedded at Fox News, but until you're in the thick of it, you have no idea how scary a place Fox News can be," Mr. Peterson said.

The journalist added that even with the unfettered access he has been given to Fox News, the news channel has been careful to protect him from situations that it deems too dangerous.

"I'm not allowed to talk to Bill O'Reilly when he's in the makeup chair," he said.

A journalist said that being embedded on Fox News programs like *Fox & Friends* was a "scary and lonely" experience.

TERROR STATUS REDUCED TO YELLOW; RIDGE URGES AMERICANS TO BUY SCOTCH TAPE

New Tobacco and Alcohol Consumption Guidelines Released for Code Yellow

The Department of Homeland Security reduced the nation's terror alert status from Orange to Yellow today, with Homeland Security Secretary Tom Ridge urging all Americans to stock up on Scotch tape rather than duct tape and to immediately destroy half the amount of water and food they keep in their homes.

"Under Code Yellow, sealing a room in your house with Scotch tape will do the trick," Mr. Ridge said. "And if you run out of tape before you're done, don't lose any sleep over it."

Mr. Ridge also gave a complete list of tobacco and alcohol guidelines for Code Yellow, urging Americans to cut back to two packs of cigarettes a day and one forty-ounce can of malt liquor before lunch.

In addition, Mr. Ridge said, Americans who have been irritably snapping at their spouses during Code Orange may now merely give them dirty looks and subject them to long, stony silences.

While the government said that the reduction in terror alert status came about because of a reduction in terrorist chatter in recent days, Professor Daniel Rutledge, chairman of the Department of Terrorist Chatter Studies at the University of Minnesota, disagrees with this assessment.

"Terrorist chatter always goes down at the end of the month," Dr. Rutledge said. "Al-Qaeda operatives are on a Friends and Extremists cellphone plan, which only gives them one thousand free minutes to make terror threats each month."

Americans rushed to buy Scotch tape after Homeland Security chief Tom Ridge (pictured) issued his latest recommendation.

KIM'S BLOG

One thing I don't understand about America—besides the lingering popularity of Whoopi Goldberg—is the Department of Homeland Security. Where did they dig up this Tom Ridge dude, that's what I'd like to know. Think about it—his main job, really, is to make Americans feel more secure. When I look at Tom Ridge, I'm like, who was their second choice for this job, a startled deer?

If I lived in America, I'd go out and buy duct tape and plastic sheeting, seal off a room in my house—and every time Tom Ridge came on TV, I would go into that room.

I've had a slightly different approach to homeland security in North Korea. I've told all of our citizens that in the event of an attack, they are to get out of their homes and run around outside in circles, like ants pouring out of an anthill that's just been smashed with a big stick.

This strategy has two main purposes. First, people who are running around in circles like ants make really tricky targets. And second, if you're being attacked, running around in circles gives you something else to occupy your mind.

Meanwhile, I'll be 9,000 feet underground in my emergency bunker, waiting for the excitement to die down. I've got enough DVDs and foodstuffs to last until 2035. Bring it on!

BUSH: WAR, MADONNA OFFICIALLY OVER

But Critics Assail Post-Madonna Planning

I n a nationally broadcast address last night, President George W. Bush pronounced the war in Iraq, as well as the singer-actress Madonna, officially over.

"The war in Iraq is over," the President simply stated, "and so is Madonna."

While Mr. Bush acknowledged that Madonna still had "pockets of listeners," he added that even they would soon disperse after listening to her new CD, *American Life.*

Around the globe, millions who had lived under the yoke of Madonna for the last twenty years poured out into the streets in spontaneous celebrations.

Customers at Tower Records on London's fabled Oxford Street tore down a life-sized cardboard cutout of the erstwhile "Material Girl" before repeatedly throwing their shoes at it.

But even as euphoria over the end of Madonna's reign spread from hemisphere to hemisphere, Dr. David Henner, who studies annoying celebrities at the University of Minnesota, cautioned that little or no thought had been given to what might eventually replace Madonna.

"In a worst-case scenario, her sudden departure could be setting the stage for Kelly Osbourne or Kelly Clarkson or some other Kelly we don't even know about yet," Dr. Henner said.

MISSION ACCOMPLISHED: Former "Material Girl" Madonna is officially over, the President announced.

CHIRAC CALLS FOR AN END TO FRENCH JOKES

Bush Blasts Proposal as "Premature"

French President Jacques Chirac today called for an "immediate cessation" of jokes about France now that the active combat phase in Iraq had concluded.

In an impassioned speech to the United Nations Security Council, Mr. Chirac said that if the time had come to lift sanctions against Iraq, "then it is also time to stop calling the French 'cheese-eating surrender monkeys.'"

In addition, Mr. Chirac asked the U.S. to reverse its decision to rename French fries "Freedom fries," arguing that the derisive renaming of that popular delicacy was currently costing France billions of euros in royalties every week.

In his most emotional appeal, Mr. Chirac asked that the U.S. stop referring to the French as "weasels" and refrain from gratuitous references to France's inexplicable love affair with the actors Jerry Lewis and Mickey Rourke.

"Get over it!" Mr. Chirac roared.

But Mr. Chirac's speech may have fallen on deaf ears at the White House, where President Bush today characterized the French President's request as "premature."

"The United States has no timetable for stopping making fun of the French," Mr. Bush said. "We'll stop ridiculing the French when we're good and ready, and not one day sooner."

When told of Mr. Bush's statement, Mr. Chirac sighed deeply and said, "I give up," to which Mr. Bush replied, chuckling, "Of course he gives up—he's French."

French President Jacques Chirac (middle) argued that jokes about France are no longer appropriate now that major combat operations in Iraq have concluded.

KIM'S BLOG

Let me talk for a second about that whole "Freedom fries" hoo-hah.

As you'll probably recall, in the run-up to the Iraq war, France decided not to support the U.S. (and if that surprised you, you're probably surprised by the plot twists on *The O.C.*, too). So some wise guy in the congressional cafeteria decided to rename French fries "Freedom fries," which led to all kinds of other, equally clever "Freedom" names. Freedom toast, Freedom kisses—it was a lot of fun for a while there! Only problem was, we here in North Korea felt a little left out.

Then it occurred to me—I don't have anything against the French, but I sure as hell have a problem with America, so why don't I rename things that have the word "American" in them? And so I did, replacing the word "American" with "Bite My Ass."

What this meant was, at our cafeteria in Pyongyang, all of a sudden we had "Bite My Ass Cheese Sandwich" on the menu. In the local movie theater, *Bite My Ass Pie 2* was showing. We redid the Lenny Kravitz version of "American Woman" so it went "Bite My Ass Woman." I have never laughed so hard in my life.

A few weeks later I got an angry letter from the American embassy in South Korea—I guess they were none too pleased about my little renaming thing. So I sent them a very apologetic letter, but I addressed it to—check it out—"The Bite My Ass Embassy, Seoul, South Korea."

I know, "real mature," but I couldn't help myself.

WINONA RYDER RETURNS IRAQI ARTIFACTS

World's Oldest Vase Found in Actress's Saks Bag

Actress Winona Ryder returned a trove of priceless Iraqi artifacts to the National Museum of Iraq today, apologizing for taking part in a wanton looting spree two weeks ago.

Ms. Ryder's role in the looting of Iraqi's national treasures had gone unnoticed until earlier this week, when U.S. officials reviewing security camera footage from the museum saw the actress moving suspiciously through the galleries with an oversized Saks Fifth Avenue shopping bag.

"We were looking at the tapes, and all of a sudden I was like, there's the chick from *Mr. Deeds*," one military official said.

The military investigators took extra time to ascertain that the person on the tape was in fact Ms. Ryder and not one of several body doubles she routinely uses to distract department store security guards.

Using various intelligence leads, the U.S. was able to track Ms. Ryder to the southern city of Basra, where she was found living in an apartment chock full of Iraqi antiquities, including what is believed to be "the world's oldest vase," according to CENTCOM spokesman Vincent Brooks.

After apologizing for taking part in the looting of Iraq's National Museum, Ms. Ryder back-tracked somewhat, saying that she was merely researching a role for an upcoming film in which she plays "a crazy actress who keeps changing her story."

U.S. officials were reportedly pleased that actress Winona Ryder (pictured) agreed to return priceless Sumerian artifacts to the National Museum of Iraq.

BUSH TO PHASE OUT ENVIRONMENT BY 2004

All Species Under Review, President Says

Just days after Christine Todd Whitman departed her post at the Environmental Protection Agency, President George W. Bush announced ambitious new plans to phase out the environment altogether by 2004.

"In addition to cutting taxes, it is the goal of

Former head of the EPA Christine Todd Whitman applauds President Bush's decision to phase out all air, water and wildlife by 2004.

this administration to cut our wasteful, bloated environment," Mr. Bush said in a speech before the Association of Indiscriminate Applauders in Washington, D.C.

While plans to eliminate the environment entirely are still being formulated, the general strategy of the White House is to phase out the environment gradually "so that hardly anyone will notice it's gone," an aide said today.

Apparently, the plan to phase out the environment may have prompted Ms. Whitman's decision to leave the EPA, since the agency's mission seemed increasingly nebulous in the absence of an environment to protect.

"Christie decided to move from the EPA to New Jersey because a year from now New Jersey will still be around," one source said.

The President's plan to eliminate the environment calls for a comprehensive review of all species currently living in the United States and the accelerated extinction of all superfluous organisms by the end of fiscal 2004.

The plan also calls for a gradual reduction of air and water, with water most likely to get the ax.

"If it comes down to choosing between air and water, the President will probably scrap water," one aide said. "After all, the Iraqis haven't had water in weeks and look how well they're doing."

GRETA VAN SUSTEREN UNDERGOES RADICAL HEAD-REPLACEMENT SURGERY

Old Head to Return to CNN in Ramped-Up Ratings War

Fox News personality Greta Van Susteren, bowing to pressure from her new bosses at Fox News Channel, had her entire head surgically replaced today, Fox News announced.

A spokesman for Fox pronounced Van Susteren's new head "a home run."

"While we were supportive of Greta's earlier plastic surgery, we felt that that procedure didn't get it done," Fox spokesman Carla Benoit told reporters.

"All of us at Fox are very excited to be working with Greta and her new, much better-looking head," Ms. Benoit said.

Although Van Susteren joins a long list of unrecognizable surgically altered celebrities that includes Roseanne, Liza Minelli, and Michael Jackson, radical head-replacement surgery is still a relatively rare option, experts say.

A costly and high-risk medical procedure, it was successfully performed for the first time three years ago, on Lewinskygate figure Linda Tripp, who successfully replaced her frightening head.

As Fox laid out plans to unveil Van Susteren's new head later this week, CNN an-nounced today that Van Susteren's original head would be returning to her old network.

CNN, where Van Susteren had toiled for years before bolting to Fox, plans to schedule what it calls "Greta's real head" against Van Susteren's new head in a much-anticipated head-to-head ratings battle.

"We wish Greta well in her new job," CNN said today in a prepared statement, "but may the best head win."

HEAD TO HEAD: Fox News' Greta Van Susteren said she is "stoked" about squaring off against her old head in a much-anticipated ratings battle with CNN.

BUSH REBUFFED BY MODEL U.N.

Pretend-Diplomats Call President's Request "Bogus"

Just days after receiving a chilly reception from the United Nations, President Bush took his appeal for Iraq aid to the Model United Nations, a group of two thousand high school students meeting in San Diego.

The Model U.N., which convenes once a year to simulate the proceedings of the world body, is primarily an educational organization and is therefore unaccustomed to requests for troops, funds, and billions of dollars in loans—precisely what the President asked the teenage delegates for today.

President Bush was reportedly blindsided by the Model U.N.'s chilly response to his speech this week.

"The United States liberated Iraq to preserve the credibility not only of the United Nations, but of the Model United Nations as well," Mr. Bush told the high school students, to muted applause.

While many in attendance seemed unmoved by the President's appeal, Mr. Bush received the frostiest reception by far from the high school students pretending to represent France and Germany.

"When he was, like, 'Give us billions of dollars and whatnot,' I was, like, 'This is bogus,'"

said Josh Greenstein, the ambassador from France.

The German ambassador, Lum Chao, echoed his French colleague's dismissive remarks about Mr. Bush's speech.

"Dude was trippin'," Mr. Chao said. "Yo, when do we go to SeaWorld?"

Speaking to CNN's Wolf Blitzer later in the day, Vice President Dick Cheney criticized the Model U.N., arguing, "If the Model U.N. does not act, then they are little more than a glorified debating society."

OPENLY EPISCOPAL MAN JOINS VILLAGE PEOPLE

Controversy Threatens to Tear Disco Band Asunder

For the first time in their three decades of existence, the disco band the Village People have inducted an openly Episcopal man, igniting a controversy that threatens to tear the fabled group asunder.

Holding a press conference in New York City today, the Construction Worker, a prominent member of the Village People since its inception in the 1970s, urged "tolerance and understanding" for its latest member, the Episcopal Guy, who joined the group over the weekend.

"From the start, the Village People have been all about inclusiveness," the Construction Worker said. "And introducing the Episcopal Guy as our latest member is part of that tradition."

While the Indian Chief and the Fireman were reportedly in agreement with the Construction Worker about including the Episcopal Guy in the band, the Policeman, the Cowboy, and the Leather-clad Guy were reportedly opposed, creating speculation that the Village People might split up into two smaller, somewhat less influential disco bands.

Meanwhile, one full day after rap impresario Sean "P. Diddy" Combs ran the New York City Marathon, Mr. Combs' posse finally crossed the finish line with a time of 30:16:27.

While the posse's finish was unimpressive compared to that of the winner, Kenyan Martin Lel, it does set a new record for best finish by a bloated entourage of leeches and parasites.

The introduction of an openly Episcopal man could split the Village People into two smaller, less influential disco bands.

UNNAMED WHITE HOUSE SOURCE DENIES LEAK

White House Denies Leaking Denial

An unnamed White House source last night vigorously denied leaking classified information about a CIA operative, sending the White House scrambling to identify the source of the leaked denial.

The unnamed source leaked a strongly worded denial of the previous leak in phone conversations with over two hundred newspaper columnists across the country.

"We are not in the business of leaking information," the unnamed source said.

Ben Trimble, a political columnist for the *Canton* (Ohio) *Star-Ledger*, attempted to STAR-69 the call in order to identify the source of the leaked denial, but to no avail.

"It wouldn't disclose the phone number or the location," Mr. Trimble said. "That kind of made me think it was Cheney."

At the White House, spokesman Scott McClellan said that the administration would launch a "full investigation" to determine the source of the leaked denials.

"If someone is out there denying leaks, that is very serious business," Mr. McClellan said. "Denying leaks is my job."

But moments after Mr. McClellan spoke, columnists received a new round of anonymous phone calls, this time denying that the White House had been the source of the earlier denials.

White House spokesman Scott McClellan said that the unnamed source who has been denying leaks remains unnamed and unknown.

As the number of anonymous leaks from the White House mounts to a dozen or more a day, newspaper columnists are increasingly signing up for the Federal "Do Not Call" list to keep unnamed White House sources from bothering them at home.

"The first couple of leaks I didn't mind," said the *Star-Ledger*'s Trimble. "But these guys keep calling me at dinnertime."

In other news, the White House acknowledged today that the President's approval numbers were slipping, but added that they are still higher than his grades at Yale.

SCIENTISTS DOUBT THE EXISTENCE OF MIRA SORVINO

Nineties Actress Joins Bigfoot, Loch Ness Monster as Product of Mass Hysteria

The actress Mira Sorvino, who at one point during the 1990s seemed to appear in every movie released by Hollywood, has all but vanished from the current entertainment scene—leading some prominent scientists to believe that she may have never existed in the first place.

"The phenomenon we call 'Mira Sorvino' is increasingly looking like a product of mass hysteria," says Dr. Simon Trullo of the University of Minnesota, who has been at the vanguard of Sorvino skeptics in the scientific community.

"Like many of my colleagues, I don't question the sincerity of those who believe that 'Mira Sorvino' exists," Dr. Trullo says. "But in the absence of any proof that she does, we can only conclude that what people think is 'Mira Sorvino' is probably something else."

A phone call to a Canton, Ohio, Blockbuster video store seemed to bear out Dr. Trullo's claim that Mira Sorvino does not exist.

Karl, the clerk who answered the phone, could not locate a video featuring Mira Sorvino anywhere in the store's inventory.

"Are you sure you don't mean Mena Suvari?" the clerk said, referring to the starlet of *American Beauty* and *American Pie* fame.

The video clerk is not alone in his confusion,

Scientists believe that the phenomenon known as Mira Sorvino may have merely been the product of mass hysteria.

since some scientists—admittedly a minority—are currently testing the hypothesis that Mira Sorvino and Mena Suvari may in fact be the same person.

"They're not," Dr. Trullo says. "The dates simply don't add up."

Some stubborn Mira Sorvino believers point to the actress's acceptance, on national television, of the Best Supporting Actress Oscar for the film *Mighty Aphrodite*—but Dr. Trullo remains unconvinced.

"Like man landing on the moon, Mira Sorvino winning that Oscar is something that many people saw on TV, yet none of them can prove really happened," Dr. Trullo says.

RUMSFELD PROPOSES MERGING IRAQ, AFGHANISTAN INTO IRAQISTAN

Ten-lane Highway Through Iran Would Unite Two War Zones

As part of his long-term goal of remaking the Middle East, Secretary of Defense Donald H. Rumsfeld today suggested merging Iraq and Afghanistan into one nation, tentatively named Iraqistan.

The merger of the two nations would result in "significant" savings, Mr. Rumsfeld said, since the cost of escalating one great big war was smaller than that of escalating two smaller wars.

To complete the merger, Mr. Rumsfeld said, a ten-lane highway through Iran would be built by the Halliburton Company at an estimated cost of $800 billion.

Explaining the choice of Halliburton, Mr. Rumsfeld said, "Halliburton has by far the most experience at being granted enormous contracts without bidding for them."

Just hours after Mr. Rumsfeld's announcement, President Mohammad Khatami of Iran objected to the Secretary of Defense's plan, particularly Mr. Rumsfeld's proposal to line the Iranian superhighway with Motel 6 and Denny's franchises.

Moments after Mr. Khatami's speech, however, Mr. Rumsfeld issued a fresh warning to the

Combining Iraq and Afghanistan into one country would mean "one less country pissed off at the U.S.," said Defense Secretary Donald Rumsfeld (left).

Iranian leader: "If Iran so much as obstructs the construction of even one Denny's or Motel 6, that will be seen as a direct threat to the sovereignty of the Iraqistanian people."

Mr. Rumsfeld, while stopping short of threatening Iran with war, said he would not rule out incorporating Iran into a new nation, tentatively named Iraqiranistan.

While some foreign policy experts worry that an Operation Iraqiranistanian Freedom might spread the U.S.'s military resources too thin, Mr. Rumsfeld identified what he called a "huge upside" of such a war: "Instead of three nations being pissed off at us, there'd just be one."

KIM'S BLOG

A frightening whack-job who laughs when he talks about invading other countries, refuses to answer questions posed to him by the press and shrouds his every move in secrecy? Throw in a goofy pair of wire-rimmed glasses, and who are we talking about?

If you guessed "Kim Jong Il," you're wrong—the correct answer is "Donald Rumsfeld."

Why yours truly is considered a menace to the universe while Rumsfeld is considered a protector of peace and freedom everywhere is one of those enduring mysteries I'll never fathom. And to make matters worse, as far as I'm concerned Rummy completely stole my act!

A couple of years ago, one of my associates from the Ministry of Retribution came running into my office with a videotape. He was like, "Kim, check this out." So I stopped playing Tetris and popped the tape into the VCR. Dude, what I saw totally blew my mind: there was Rummy, in a Pentagon briefing, cackling away like a maniac and bisecting the air with a chopping motion lifted directly from the Korean art of self-defense known as Hapkido—in other words, my fucking hand gestures. It totally freaked me out.

My advisors said I should sue the bastard for copyright infringement, but I've never been a litigious guy. Like so many other disputes, this is just one of those things that I think is best settled by nuclear war.

IRAQI INFORMATION MINISTER MOVES TO AOL TIME WARNER

Named Company's Official Spokesman

Muhammad Said al-Sahhaf, the former Information Minister of Iraq, was named today as the new official corporate spokesman for AOL Time Warner in New York.

Mr. al-Sahhaf, who just days ago had been saying that coalition troops were nowhere near the gates of Baghdad, had generally positive things to say about AOL Time Warner's prospects in today's competitive media environment.

"The merger of AOL and Time Warner was the most successful merger in the history of the media world," said Mr. al-Sahhaf, wearing his trademark beret. "All you have to do is take a look at the value of our executives' stock options—they're worth untold billions."

Mr. al-Sahhaf disputed reports that the company was desperately trying to raise cash by selling assets such as its two Atlanta sports teams.

"No parts of this company are for sale—in fact, we'd like to go on a buying spree right now," Mr. al-Sahhaf said. "That's what companies do when their bottom lines are gushing cash, which is precisely what ours is doing."

Mr. al-Sahhaf also took issue with reports that Ted Turner, a major AOL TW stockholder, felt alienated from the company: "That is insane! Ted Turner is deliriously happy! At our last board meeting he was purring like a little kitten. Ask anyone who was there."

While many on Wall Street welcomed Mr. al-Sahhaf's upbeat assessment of the company's prospects, Ira Hogan of Credit Suisse First Boston lowered his recommendation on AOL TW to "sell," primarily because of the company's decision to hire Mr. al-Sahhaf.

Asked to comment on Mr. Hogan's move, Mr. al-Sahhaf replied, "That gangster bastard will meet with a fiery doom of his own making."

AOL Time Warner anticipates a "banner year for revenues and profits," the former Iraqi Information Minister confirmed.

OBESITY MAY BE AMERICA'S SECRET WEAPON IN WAR ON TERROR

Americans Taking Up More Space, Leaving Less for Evildoers

Call it Survival of the Fattest. Obesity, long thought to be one of America's nagging problems, may be something else entirely—its secret weapon in the war on terror.

A new study out today offers evidence that as America grows fatter, it may actually offer a stiffer challenge to terrorists who wish to infiltrate the U.S. for nefarious purposes.

"The average American today is between fifty and seventy pounds overweight," said Dr.

Terrorists (pictured above) now have to gain between 100 and 150 extra pounds to successfully infiltrate the U.S. population, experts say.

Charles Reardon, author of the study. "That means that a terrorist who hopes to fit in here would have to eat like a pig to do so."

The end result, Dr. Reardon said, is that any terrorist trying to pass himself off as an obese American would wind up in terrible cardiovascular shape, making him easier for law enforcement to chase in a foot race.

"We're going to be looking at a whole new generation of flabby, easily winded terrorists," Dr. Reardon said.

In addition, tougher restrictions on obese passengers by such airlines as Southwest—who requires that obese flyers buy two seats instead of one—will have the effect of "crowding out" would-be terrorists.

"All in all, Americans are taking up more room, leaving less room for evildoers," Dr. Reardon said.

Dr. Reardon said he hoped that the results of the survey would convince Americans that eating more and exercising less were their patriotic duties.

The study, which was the culmination of six months of intensive research, was commissioned by the Frito Lay Company in conjunction with Kentucky Fried Chicken.

 KIM'S BLOG

Not a day goes by that Bush or Cheney or Rice or some other imperialist stooge accuses me of starving my people. Even Colin Powell took his best shot at yours truly, telling reporters, "You can't eat plutonium."

Well, all I can say to that is, don't say you can't do something if you've never tried it. I keep a chunk of plutonium in my fridge, and when I'm looking for a little midnight snack it's usually the first thing I grab, and not just because it glows in the dark—it's darn tasty.

But I guess what really honks me off about the "starving my people" business is that in America they're doing just the opposite: *feeding* their people to death! The average McDonald's meal has enough calories to feed an average North Korean family for three years, and longer than that if you throw in a McFlurry.

I think it's highly ironic that America, with its wall-to-wall Trimspa, Atkins and Bowflex infomercials would take me to task for keeping the people of North Korea thin and trim, but go figure. Like so much else in my relations with the U.S., their attitude toward me can be boiled down to one word: envy. All I can say is, don't hate the player, hate the game.

BUSH MAY LACK GENE FOR HUMAN SPEECH

President Has No Comment

A team of genetic scientists stunned the world today by revealing that President George W. Bush may lack the gene necessary for human speech.

The scientists, who had been studying the genetic differences between humans and chimps, made the discovery about the President almost by accident, a spokesman for the group said.

"We happened to be looking at the blood work from the President's recent physical," said the spokesman, Dr. Alvin Kunen of the University of Minnesota. "We found extremely high potassium levels, indicating a banana-rich diet rarely found in humans."

Prompted by the banana clue, scientists probed the President's DNA further and found "no evidence" of the gene that enables humans to speak.

From the White House, the President had no comment.

But even as some in the administration angrily questioned the scientists' findings—arguing that the President often said things—Dr. Kunen said that many nonhuman primates were capable of producing basic, "speech-like" utterances.

"In our experiments, we were able to teach a female baboon named Bonny to say such things as 'tax cut,' 'evildoer,' and 'regime change,'" Dr.

Scientists believe they have found a genetic explanation for the President's inability to create human speech.

Kunen said. "This should not be confused with actual human speech."

In a related finding, the scientists said that former President Bill Clinton possessed an "abnormal double-gene" for human speech, meaning that it was "virtually impossible to get him to shut up."

Mr. Clinton's DNA was culled during his second term in office, when the former President's genetic material was widely disseminated.

$87 BILLION FOR IRAQ SPENT IN FIRST TWO DAYS

Additional $87 Billion Sought

Two days after Congress granted the White House $87 billion for continuing operations in Iraq, the White House revealed that the money had been completely spent over the weekend.

"We are, quite frankly, disappointed that the eighty-seven billion dollars did not last a little longer," said White House spokesman Scott McClellan. "Having said that, we are confident that the next $87 billion will be money well spent."

Mr. McClellan added that the White House would seek an additional $87 billion to fund continuing operations in Iraq through next Wednesday.

The White House, anticipating criticism from congressional Democrats, conceded today that Iraq was turning out to be more expensive than first estimated, but blamed the exorbitant price tag on the high cost of food service at Baghdad International Airport.

"Currently, a cheese sandwich and a Pepsi at Baghdad International cost twenty-eight dollars," Mr. McClellan said, adding that the airport's food service providers, the Halliburton Company, were working hard to bring those costs down.

Democratic presidential candidate Sen. John Kerry (D-Mass.) today blasted the two-day expenditure of $87 billion, telling reporters in New Hampshire, "Given the way this has turned out, I am fairly certain that I would change my vote on the appropriations bill, if I could remember which way I voted on it."

On NBC's *Meet the Press*, National Security Advisor Condoleezza Rice urged approval of the additional eighty-seven billion dollars in funding, arguing, "Not providing another $87 billion would make a mockery of the $87 billion we just spent."

On other matters, Dr. Rice added that the U.S. had no intention of invading North Korea, but said that verbally threatening North Korea remained a viable and less expensive option.

Privately, President Bush acknowledged that he was "surprised" that the $87 billion for Iraq did not last longer than two days.

CHENEY EXPANDING EVEN FASTER THAN ECONOMY

Creates 20,000 Jobs for Halliburton in Last Quarter

The White House had yet another piece of good economic news to trumpet over the weekend, announcing that Vice President Dick Cheney expanded even faster than the U.S. economy in the quarter just ended.

"Our economic policy, including our program of tax cuts for the highest income brackets, have resulted in the most dramatic expansion of a Vice President in U.S. history," President Bush said in his weekly radio address on Saturday.

While President Bush acknowledged that many Americans had yet to reap positive benefits from Mr. Cheney's explosive growth, he said that it was only a matter of time before the Vice President's surging wealth trickled down to the rest of the country.

According to figures released by the White House, Vice President Cheney expanded at a torrid 11.2 percent rate in the last quarter, creating over 20,000 new jobs, most of them for the Halliburton Company.

While economists expressed amazement at Mr. Cheney's unprecedented growth rate, however, some doubted that his dramatic expansion could be sustained.

But Charles Donner, chief economist for Credit Suisse First Boston, predicted that the

Vice President Dick Cheney is on a pace to become the world's largest economy, latest numbers indicate.

next quarter will also be strong for the Vice President, with the completion of an oil and gas pipeline leading directly from the former Soviet republic of Uzbekistan directly into Mr. Cheney himself.

"With the completion of that pipeline, Dick Cheney will become the second-largest economy in the world," Mr. Donner said.

GE STILL PAYING FOR RETIRED CEO'S CRACK, HO'S

Jack Welch's Posse Swells to 400

In the latest tale of CEO greed to hit Wall Street, outraged investors learned today that General Electric is still paying for former CEO Jack Welch's crack, ho's and 400-homie-strong posse.

The revelations, which appeared in divorce papers filed by estranged wife Jane Welch, drew howls from corporate governance watchdogs.

"It may have been appropriate for GE to foot the bill for Welch's crack, ho's and posse while he was still running the company," said Peter Kenney of the Institute for Corporate Responsibility. "But certainly not in retirement."

Mr. Kenney was especially critical of the size of Welch's retirement posse, which he termed "extraordinary" even by *Fortune* 500 standards.

"A retired CEO really should be able to get by with twenty or thirty homies at most," Mr. Kenney said.

But for his part, Mr. Welch was unrepentant, appearing at a press conference with his wife, former *Harvard Business Review* editor Suzy Wetlaufer, and his 400-member posse, decked out in Prada suits and expensive designer eyeglasses.

"I represent honies with money fly guys with gems," Welch said, adding, "Drive with the tints that be thirty-five percent."

The outcry about Welch's retirement perks

Former General Electric CEO Jack Welch defended retirement benefits that include crack, ho's, and a bloated posse of fly guys.

came amid revelations that his West Coast rival, Bill Gates, had just increased the size of his posse to 500.

The swelling size of the two corporate honchos' posses raised fears among many in the financial community about a potentially volatile East Coast–West Coast confrontation between the CEOs, their homies, and money fly guys with gems.

COPYCAT MINERS TRAP SELVES FOR MOVIE DEAL

Hoping for Heroic Rescue, 10 Percent of the Gross

Apparently inspired by the impressive sums that Hollywood has offered the rescued miners in western Pennsylvania, a group of nine miners in western Indiana have intentionally trapped themselves in a mine in the hopes of scoring a movie deal.

"My clients are hoping for a heroic rescue and a percentage of the adjusted gross," said Ian Whitestone of the William Morris Agency, who is representing the self-trapped miners in their Hollywood dealings.

The stakes are high for the so-called "copycat" miners, who are trying to land not only a movie deal but also seven-figure paydays for trapped-miner video games, action figures, and a possible sitcom or Broadway musical.

But with several Hollywood studios and broadcast networks taking "pitches" from the trapped miners via conference calls yesterday, the initial results were somewhat less than encouraging.

"I heard their whole story, and I thought they needed a new ending," said Stacy Conant, a production vice president at Paramount Pictures. "Right now, all that happens is they get rescued. I was like, So what? It seemed a little tired to me."

Bob Littlesmith, a programming executive at ABC, agreed: "Their whole pitch kind of fell off at the end. It definitely needs a twist. Maybe they could eat each other or something."

For his part, William Morris' Whitestone said his clients would do whatever it takes to score a deal based on their self-inflicted ordeal.

"My clients are completely open to the idea of not being rescued, and are currently exploring the idea of eating each other," Mr. Whitestone said.

Hollywood executives called the stories pitched by copycat miners "derivative."

BUSH: SADDAM BOUGHT GERANIUMS, NOT URANIUM

White House Defends War Decision Based on Typo

In an extraordinary retraction of key elements in his last State of the Union address, President George W. Bush revealed today that Iraqi strongman Saddam Hussein did not attempt to buy uranium in Africa, as earlier alleged, but merely geraniums.

"As I was reading the speech to the nation, I should have caught that typo," the President told reporters today. "My bad."

While the news about the uranium/geranium goof stunned diplomatic circles, Mr. Bush remained resolute about his decision to go to war, arguing that buying geraniums, while not as potentially dangerous as buying uranium, still represented a "suspicious" activity on the part of the Iraqi madman.

"The question we have to ask is, who was he buying these geraniums for?" Mr. Bush said. "Was he buying them for Osama bin Laden or Kim Jong Il or some other evildoer? Luckily, we'll never find out."

Mr. Bush said that, thanks to Operation Iraqi Freedom, "Saddam Hussein is no longer free to terrorize the world with his evil flower-buying sprees."

While the President may have been trying to quell international criticism, his comments instead sparked more controversy, as French President Jacques Chirac challenged the U.S. to find evidence of geraniums anywhere in Iraq.

In response, Secretary of Defense Donald H. Rumsfeld said that while the U.S. had yet to turn up any concrete evidence of geraniums, U.S. forces had uncovered several "suspicious" empty flowerpots outside of Basra.

Asked by reporters about the flowerpots, Mr. Bush gave a thumbs-up gesture and said, "Mission accomplished."

Saddam may have sought deadly geraniums (pictured) in Africa.

QWEST SELLS YELLOW PAGES FOR $7 BILLION; HIGHEST PRICE EVER PAID FOR FREE ITEM FOUND IN DRIVEWAY

Phone Book's Price Tag Surprises Many at Company's Yard Sale

Embattled telecom giant Qwest Communications sold the Yellow Pages yesterday for $7.05 billion, believed to be the highest price ever paid for a free item found in the driveway.

The surprising ten-figure sale occurred at a company yard sale held to avert a bankruptcy filing, said Roy Helton, a Qwest employee who helped run the yard sale.

"We were just throwing stuff in the back of our Explorer to bring it to the yard sale, and my wife said, 'Hey, how about those Yellow Pages?'" Mr. Helton said, referring to a phone directory that had just been delivered and was still sitting in the driveway.

"So I said, 'Sure, what the hey,' but I never thought in a million years that anyone would buy it," Mr. Helton said. "Nobody ever pays for the Yellow Pages—they're free."

Contrary to his expectations, Mr. Helton said, the Yellow Pages were snapped up at the yard sale by the Carlyle Group and Welsh, Carson, Anderson & Stowe.

"To say I was surprised that they paid several billion for a phone book is putting it mildly," he said. "There were perfectly good copying ma-

Qwest stunned analysts with the $7 billion it received for a phone book it sold at a company yard sale.

chines and printers sitting right next to it on the table."

On Wall Street, telecom analyst Carla Bollinger of Credit Suisse First Boston said that the $7 billion price tag garnered by the Yellow Pages may inspire troubled companies to sell other free items found in driveways, such as supermarket circulars and Chinese takeout menus.

U.S. SENDS UDAY AND QUSAY'S HEADS ON 21-CITY TOUR

"Not Gloating," Cautions Rumsfeld

In an extraordinary attempt to convince the Iraqi people that fallen madmen Uday and Qusay Hussein are dead, the U.S. today announced plans to send the heads of the evil brothers on a twenty-one-city tour of Iraq later this week.

The despised heads are scheduled to make stops in Mosul, Basra, Tikrit and the oil-rich city of Kirkuk, returning to Baghdad at the end of August.

At the Pentagon, Secretary of Defense Donald Rumsfeld denied that the extensive showings of the Hussein brothers' heads constituted gloating on the part of the U.S., and said that T-shirts, bumper stickers and beverage cups bearing the images of the two evildoers would be "tasteful."

Dismissing charges of gloating, Mr. Rumsfeld said, "It would be gloating if I danced a jig around the heads while stark naked, and there are no plans at the present time for me to do that."

The upcoming tour must convince a highly skeptical Iraqi populace that the two Hussein brothers are in fact dead, as a recent poll finds that 94 percent of all Iraqis believe that the heads shown on TV were not those of Uday and Qusay, but were instead part of a really bad makeover show.

In other dismemberment news, the right

In Baghdad, an Iraqi citizen responded to the news that Uday and Qusay Hussein's heads would go on a twenty-one-city tour.

hand of Senator Hillary Clinton (D-N.Y.) fell off today after a three-hour book signing of her bestseller, *Living History*, at a San Francisco Barnes & Noble bookstore.

Ms. Clinton was rushed to an area hospital for treatment while her hand remained at the store and signed books for another forty-five minutes.

BASEBALL TAKES BOLD STEPS TO ALIENATE REMAINING FANS

Commissioner Selig Declares All Future Games "a Tie"

Baseball Commissioner Bud Selig announced today that Major League Baseball is about to take a series of bold steps with the stated goal of alienating its remaining fans forever.

"At baseball stadiums across the country, it is too hard to find parking spots, and one must wait on long lines for beer and bathrooms," Mr. Selig said. "All of these problems have the same source: simply put, the sport has too many fans."

As Mr. Selig's first step in his plan to achieve contraction of baseball's fan base, the commissioner declared all games to be played for the remainder of the 2002 season a tie.

"The score's tied, fans, so please, don't watch the game," Mr. Selig said. "Watch wrestling or NASCAR instead."

In addition, Mr. Selig said, it would now take nine strikes to strike out a batter instead of the traditional three, a rule-change aimed at making the average game six and a half hours long.

These changes, along with the outlawing of home runs and stolen bases, should reduce baseball's popularity to the level of badminton or curling, Mr. Selig promised.

In addition, the commissioner said, the traditional seventh-inning stretch will now entail the playing of a thirty-minute section from rocker Lou Reed's album *Metal Machine Music*, during which time stadium ushers will move about the stands poking spectators with sharp sticks.

In an effort to alienate its few remaining fans, Major League Baseball plans to make ticketholders wait for hours and then spray them with fire hoses before permitting them to enter the stadium.

KIM'S BLOG

One thing you may not know about yours truly is that over the years I have been an enormous fan of American baseball. Fidel Castro turned me onto the sport many years ago at a meeting of the Council of Evil (this was before we changed our name to the scarier-sounding "Axis"— "Council" made us sound like a fucking trade association).

A couple of years later, Castro convinced me to join a rotisserie league he was in. During baseball season, I used to spend almost as much time updating the stats of my rotisserie team as I did restarting dormant nuclear reactors. I used to take a lot of shit for this around the office, I can tell you that!

In recent years, though, much of the fun of the sport of baseball has been drained out of it, largely due to the widespread use of steroids. When players who might have hit only ten home runs a year now routinely hit fifty or sixty, the uniqueness of the achievement is gone. It's like, what would be the fun of having ninety long-range ballistic missiles if you found out that South Korea had ninety big ones, too? It's enough to make you want to blow up the world.

So lately I've been gravitating away from baseball and watching women's tennis. That Anna Kournikova is some hot hot hottie! I wonder if she's with anyone.

PETER JENNINGS RESPONDS TO PAY CUT WITH NEWS CUT

His Salary Slashed, ABC Anchor Plans to Read 50 Percent Less News

ABC's *World News Tonight* anchor Peter Jennings said today that if the network proceeds with plans to cut his salary, he would respond by reading 50 percent less news during each evening telecast.

"Mr. Jennings acknowledges the network's desire to curtail costs in its news division," a spokesman for Mr. Jennings said today. "But if his salary is slashed as has been proposed, Mr. Jennings will respond by reading the news in a totally lazy-ass way."

According to his spokesman, Mr. Jennings will also refuse to read news stories taking place on more than two continents in the same telecast.

Under this plan, Mr. Jennings might read news stories about Afghanistan and Venezuela in the same evening, for example, but refuse to report any news about America.

"In an ideal world, it would be great if Peter were willing to report events that are happening in America," ABC News President David Westin acknowledged. "But we have to cut corners somewhere, and if that means no news about America, so be it."

Contacted at his office in New York, Mr. Jennings said that he would no longer feel obligated to speak in complete sentences, or even grammatical ones.

Peter Jennings has threatened to read 50 percent less news if ABC insists on slashing his salary.

"You gets what you pays for," Mr. Jennings said.

In addition, Mr. Jennings indicated that he would not make an effort to dress up for his nightly news broadcasts anymore, but would instead dig into his closet full of raunchy-slogan T-shirts.

Jennings' collection of smutty T-shirts has been legendary in news circles ever since last summer, when the esteemed newsman showed up at a party in East Hampton wearing a shirt that read ANCHORMEN DO IT UNDER THEIR DESKS.

BUSH EYES SWEATER-RICH KASHMIR AS KEY SOURCE OF STATIC ELECTRICITY

"No Blood for Wool," D.C. Protesters Chant

Just days after the worst electrical blackout in U.S. history, the Bush administration is focusing new attention on the contested region of Kashmir, the world's leading producer of wool for cashmere sweaters, as a sustainable source of static electricity.

With the U.S. electrical grid overtaxed and with public opposition to nuclear power plants on the rise, Mr. Bush has become an enthusiastic supporter of using cashmere sweaters to create substantial amounts of static electricity going forward, aides say.

Kashmir, a region long contested by India and Pakistan, had been on the administration's back burner before the blackout, but all that changed Monday when Mr. Bush announced that he was "very concerned about the freedom of Kashmir's goat population."

"If those goats and their precious wool are threatened, that threatens the world's supply of cashmere sweaters and static electricity," Mr. Bush told reporters at the White House. "And that directly threatens the security of the United States of America."

In Washington, rumors that the U.S. might divert forces currently in Liberia and send them to Kashmir instead to secure the region's coveted goats sparked massive protests, as marchers headed for the Capitol chanting, "No blood for wool."

On the Fox News Channel, Vice President Dick Cheney clarified the administration's position on Kashmir, telling Fox's Brit Hume, "The United States must decrease its dependence on foreign wool."

"The only way to do that," Mr. Cheney added, "is by seizing vast quantities of foreign wool with overwhelming military force."

NO BLOOD FOR WOOL: Precious Kashmiri goats are seen as a plentiful source of static electricity.

GREENSPAN: NUMBER OF AMERICANS PRETENDING TO WORK SURGED IN FEBRUARY

Jump in Internet Casino, Porn Usage Signals Economic Recovery, Fed Chief Testifies

I n testimony before the U.S. Senate today, Federal Reserve Board Chairman Alan Greenspan said that the number of Americans pretending to work at the office jumped in February, more proof that an economic recovery is underway.

The number of Americans trying to look busy in their cubicles while doing no work whatsoever surged 17 percent, an extremely strong increase, Greenspan said.

"The members of the labor force who paid extensive visits to Internet casino and pornography sites in lieu of doing work-related tasks increased at an unprecedented rate last month," Greenspan said.

"Their willingness to shirk their duties in order to play blackjack or look at naked people is a sign of unexpected strength in the job market," the Fed chief added.

Greenspan went on to say that the number of American workers using valuable office time to visit Internet sites dedicated to the World Wrestling Federation, the Paris Hilton sex videos, and what he termed "24-hour sorority shower-cams" also surged in February.

Greenspan's testimony to the Senate was not entirely upbeat, however.

In a comment that surprised several of the senators, the Fed chief warned that some high-speed Internet users may watch online pornography "too quickly to really enjoy it."

"With the advent of DSL and other high-speed Internet technologies, pornography customers may find that things fly by too fast to be fully appreciated," Greenspan told the senators.

Porn consumption in the workplace has surged to record levels, Greenspan told Congress.

"On the positive side, less time spent watching pornography will give the habitual porn consumer more time for other tasks, such as studying job statistics and money supply, and determining the future direction of the Fed discount rate," Greenspan said.

KIM'S BLOG

Question: how come when Alan Greenspan talks, everyone listens, and when I talk, no one listens?

It's not like one of us is a whole lot taller than the other. And it's not like one of us wears glasses that are way too big for his head and the other one doesn't. So what does Alan Greenspan have that I don't have?

Before you think that I'm being paranoid again, here's an example of things Greenspan and I have said on the *exact same day,* and you tell me which is more worth paying attention to:

Greenspan: In the absence of the gold standard, there is no way to protect savings from confiscation through inflation.

Me: I will engulf the world in a scorching sea of fire.

Greenspan: How do we know when irrational exuberance has unduly escalated asset values, which then become subject to unexpected and prolonged contractions as they have in Japan over the past decade?

Me: I have my finger on the button right now. Don't think that I won't push it!

Greenspan: Evaluating shifts in balance sheets generally, and in asset prices particularly, must be an integral part of the development of monetary policy.

Me: Be afraid! Be very afraid!

So, there you have it. Why do people listen to Greenspan instead of me? Well, for one thing, Alan Greenspan is married to Andrea Mitchell of NBC News, and I'm not, so I guess in the end it's all about who you know. Note to self: marry Andrea Mitchell of NBC News.

ATHLETE WITHOUT COMPELLING PERSONAL DRAMA EXPELLED FROM OLYMPICS

Skier Concealed Adversity-Free Past From Officials, NBC

A member of the U.S. Olympic ski team was disqualified from competition today when it was learned that he did not have a sufficiently compelling human story line to exploit on the NBC telecast of the worldwide sporting event.

Tom Bergen, the expelled skier, was not raised by a single mother, never had a career-threatening injury and did not overcome a personal tragedy of any kind before making the Olympic ski team, U.S. Olympic officials revealed today.

"Had Tom been involved in an organ donation, as either a donor or a recipient, that would have been acceptable to us," ski team spokesman Sandy Harrell told reporters. "However, he was not."

According to sources close to the ski team, Bergen had concealed the fact that he comes from an intact middle-class family who never lost their home to a flood, tornado, or typhoon.

But what may have sealed Bergen's doom, sources said, was his utter lack of a gravely ill family member to win a medal for.

"Tom did his best to hide his background from team officials," one source said. "But when the truth came out, he was finished."

Speaking to reporters in Salt Lake City, NBC Sports Chairman Dick Ebersol was even less charitable, terming Bergen's actions "a reprehensible betrayal."

"We do our best to check out all of the athletes to make sure that their backgrounds are full of compelling human drama, but we can't catch everything," Ebersol said. "This is a case of one really bad guy exploiting the system."

DOWNHILL: Skier "flagrantly lied" about his intact middle-class family, Olympics officials confirmed.

VICTIMS OF EMINEM'S LATEST VERBAL ASSAULTS AGREE TO MEND THEIR WAYS

Lynne Cheney, Moby, Thousands of Others Take Rapper's Criticisms to Heart

A diverse collection of celebrities, political figures, and family members who were singled out for vituperative attack in *The Eminem Show*, the hot-selling new CD by the rapper Eminem, announced today that they would attempt to mend their ways in accordance with Eminem's criticisms.

"Eminem pointed out a number of things I did that were hypocritical and wrongheaded," said Lynne V. Cheney, wife of Vice President Dick Cheney. "Upon reflection, I now see that he is absolutely right—and I want to offer my sincerest apology."

"It is my hope," Mrs. Cheney continued, "that if I work hard enough to improve my behavior, I will someday earn Eminem's respect."

Mrs. Cheney's decision to take Eminem's profane attack in the spirit of constructive criticism was echoed by the electronic musician Moby.

"I never realized how lame I was until I heard Eminem astutely mention it on his CD," Moby said. "He's really given me a lot to think about—and to work on."

Eminem, however, remained unmoved by his victims' contrite statements, issuing a state-

Electronic musician Moby (pictured) said he would take Eminem's critiques to heart.

ment of his own in which he repeated his oft-stated desire that they contract incurable diseases and die.

"We hear you," Mrs. Cheney said.

The meeting of Eminem's victims, numbering in the thousands, filled the Los Angeles Convention Center over the past three days to overflow capacity, snarling traffic throughout the downtown area.

The meeting featured motivational speakers and several educational workshops with names like "How to Make Eminem Like You More" and "If Eminem Says You're a Ho, You Probably Are."

KIM'S BLOG

As everyone in North Korea knows, my love of hip-hop music runs deep. A few years ago, I had to make the choice between being dictator of North Korea or pursuing a career as a rapper, and I've never faced a tougher decision in my life. I think I made the right choice, but hip-hop still exerts a powerful tug on my soul.

In fact, a couple of years ago when I was heading for a summit with South Korea, I thought to myself, "I'm so misunderstood by the rest of the world—I wonder if it would help if I expressed myself by doing a little rapping?"

Like most of the stuff I do that would make people really like me and think I'm cool, my rapping at that summit was completely ignored by the Western media. But here's a little taste:

Yo, mama, I'm da bomb
Play my tunes on the jukes, yo
Cuz I got the nukes, yo
Yo, mama, I'm da bomb
Gonna reprocess fuel rods
And blow up da schoolyards
Cuz mama, I'm da bomb
If you beg to differ, wait
Watch me proliferate
I'm da bomb, yo, I'm da bomb, yo, etc.

This song shot up to number one in North Korea (remaining there for eighty weeks), but has yet to be played even *once* in America. When I take over the U.S., the first thing I'm going to fix is those stale FM playlists. They totally keep new artists from being heard, which if you ask me really blows.

RIDGE WARNS AMERICANS NOT TO SWIM TOO SOON AFTER EATING

"Wait at Least Half an Hour," Homeland Security Chief Indicates in New Alert

Tom Ridge, Director of the Office of Homeland Security, issued a "high alert" for all Americans today, warning them not to swim too soon after consuming a meal.

"If you jump in the pool right after eating, you could get serious cramps," Mr. Ridge told reporters in the Washington, D.C., press briefing. "You should wait at least half an hour."

"You don't want to wind up like the Johnson boy down the street," Ridge added. "Last summer, he practically drowned."

Director Ridge also issued an alert, effective for an indefinite period of time, warning Americans against eating spicy food, such as pizza or chili dogs, right before bedtime.

"You could wind up having terrible nightmares," Ridge said. "I don't know how many times I have to tell you this."

Ridge's wide-ranging alert covered other imminent dangers to the American people, such as sitting too close to the television, going out in cold weather with wet hair, and roughhousing on the sofa with siblings.

"To all Americans who are currently horsing around on their sofas with their brothers or sisters, I say the following: don't make me come over there," Ridge said.

Ridge went on to say that those who disre-

Homeland Security chief Tom Ridge demonstrates "a simple thing each and every one of us can do" to ward off vampires.

gard his alert run the risk of being grounded next weekend, and will not be able to come along when he takes the rest of the country to the movies and bowling.

At the conclusion of his press conference, Mr. Ridge issued a new alert to a sound technician carrying a boom microphone.

"Watch it," Mr. Ridge told the technician. "You could put an eye out with that thing."

BUSH WANTED TO INVADE IRAQ BACK IN COLLEGE

Hated Saddam While at Yale, Frat Brother Says

President George W. Bush wanted to invade Iraq back when he was a college student at Yale University, a former fraternity brother of the President revealed today.

"I wasn't the least bit surprised when we attacked Iraq last year," said Charles "Whiffy" Wiffington, a Delta Kappa Epsilon brother of the President's in the late 1960s. "This is something George has wanted to do since he was a freshman."

Mr. Wiffington said that Mr. Bush first brought up the notion of regime change in Iraq during halftime at a Harvard-Yale football game in New Haven.

"Yale had just pulled ahead of Harvard by a field goal," Mr. Wiffington remembered. "And George turned to me and said, 'Whiffy, Saddam's gotta go.'"

Although Mr. Hussein was merely a functionary in the Baath Party when Mr. Bush was at Yale, Mr. Bush remarked at numerous frat parties that the Iraqi might someday seize power, become evil, and need to be toppled, Mr. Wiffington said.

"At DKE, all we wanted to do was have bodacious keggers and meet girls, but all George could talk about was Saddam," Mr. Wiffington remembered. "We were like, 'George, cool it.'"

Mr. Wiffington said that after Mr. Bush was elected President of DKE his senior year, he proposed that the fraternity invade Iraq unilaterally.

"We had to talk him down from that," Mr. Wiffington said. "We were like, let's T.P. the Princeton bus instead."

President George W. Bush (pictured above) wanted to strike Saddam Hussein back when he was an undergraduate at Yale, friends say.

81

JUNE 17 NAMED "ATHLETES OBEY THE LAW DAY"

For 24 Hours Sports Stars Must Abide by Laws That Govern Rest of Us

June 17 has been designated Athletes Obey the Law Day, a twenty-four-hour period in which professional sports stars are being asked "to voluntarily comply with the laws that govern ordinary people."

"For one day, we are asking athletes not to drive under the influence of alcohol, crack, marijuana, cocaine, or mushrooms," said a press release for the June 17 event, "and not to abuse, harass, beat up, key the car of, or burn down the house of wives, ex-wives, girlfriends, ex-girlfriends, business managers, accountants, or Halle Berry."

But the June 17 event faces stiff opposition from the athletes, who claim that obeying the law even for one day would be onerous and unfeasible.

"Athletes already have to obey a lot of rules on the field," said Gavin Herrick, leader of an NFL players' group. "Now, on top of that, we've got to obey the law off the field? I don't think so!"

In related news, a majority of Americans fear that they will someday be the victim of an athlete's wrath after an unfortunate encounter in a restaurant, bar, hotel, disco, nightclub, clothing store, parking lot or airport lounge.

When asked, "How worried are you that you

Former NBA star Dennis Rodman was an outspoken critic of the controversial "Athletes Obey the Law Day."

may be attacked by a professional athlete in the next twelve months," 42 percent replied, "Somewhat worried"; 29 percent replied, "Very worried"; 28 percent replied, "Very, very worried"; and 1 percent replied, "I am being attacked by an athlete at this very moment."

BUSH: SADDAM STILL CAPTURED

Approval Ratings Resurge on Reannouncement

In a nationally televised address, President George W. Bush announced on Sunday that former Iraqi strongman Saddam Hussein was "still captured."

"Saddam Hussein remains very much in U.S. custody, as he has been for the last two weeks," President Bush said. "To Mr. Saddam Hussein, our message is clear: You aren't going anywhere, Mr. Saddam Hussein."

The President said that he chose to reannounce the capture of the Iraqi madman on Sunday because that day marked the two-week anniversary of Saddam's arrest in Tikrit.

"Today is a day for all Americans to remember that great and special day that occurred two weeks ago," Mr. Bush reiterated.

President Bush's approval ratings, which had leveled off somewhat over the past week, resurged after the reannouncement of Saddam's capture.

Those political dividends suggest that the White House may carry through on a controversial plan devised by chief political strategist Karl Rove to reannounce the capture of Saddam Hussein every Monday, Wednesday and Friday.

But political scientist David McCrory of the University of Minnesota warned that reannouncing the capture of the former Iraqi dictator on such a regular basis carries with it certain risks.

"Worst case scenario, people start tuning Mr. Bush out, like they do with Tom Ridge," he said.

Another proposal put forward by Mr. Rove is the so-called "catch and release" plan, in which Saddam Hussein would be released every few days, allowed to run away about fifteen yards and then recaptured by U.S. troops once more.

President Bush announcing Saddam Hussein's capture for the forty-seventh time last night.

IRAQIS FAIL TO LOVE RAYMOND

Setback for Pentagon Planners

The Pentagon today acknowledged that their attempt to introduce an American-style sitcom to post-Saddam Iraq had been a dismal failure, as Iraqis expressed their overwhelming disapproval of the CBS hit *Everybody Loves Raymond*.

"We were operating under the assumption

The Shiites' hatred of Raymond runs deep, U.S. administrators in Iraq concede.

that everybody, indeed, loves Raymond," Secretary of Defense Donald H. Rumsfeld told reporters. "Apparently, plenty of people hate Raymond, especially in the Shiite south."

In Shiite strongholds like Basra where the program debuted over the weekend, Iraqis watched the sitcom in stony silence, seething as if mocked by the raucous laugh track.

"Why do they let that idiot [Doris Roberts] in their house?" said a visibly angry Hassan El-Medfaai, 47. "If this is what democracy will bring, I'll have none of it."

Sources inside the Pentagon blamed the decision to broadcast *Raymond* on the advice of Iraqi exiles who had enjoyed the sitcom on American Airlines while jetting back and forth between London and Washington.

The discovery that Iraqis do not love Raymond is only the latest in a series of setbacks for the Pentagon planners, who last month unsuccessfully attempted to introduce Sara Lee breakfast treats to Iraq.

"Whoever said 'nobody doesn't like Sara Lee' never asked the Shiites," Mr. Rumsfeld acknowledged at the time.

The Pentagon will make one more attempt to introduce Western culture to Iraq next week by broadcasting the eighties dance single "Everybody Wang Chung Tonight" on a twenty-four-hour-a-day basis.

"If I had to guess, by the end of next week every citizen of Iraq will be wang chunging," Mr. Rumsfeld said. "But I've been wrong before."

KIM'S BLOG

When people ask me what's the best thing about North Korea being a closed society, it doesn't even take me a nanosecond to come up with an answer: "We don't have any American sitcoms here."

Oh, I know, it's an easy target. Everyone likes to complain about sitcoms, just the way some people like to bitch about a near-total absence of food. But even so, I see sitcoms for the scourge that they are because I see what the introduction of sitcoms has done to my neighbor, China.

People in the West don't know this, but China has gone absolutely sitcom-crazy since the introduction of them to the mainland back in the mid-1990s. I can't go to a nuclear summit there without President Hu Jintao saying "Kiss my grits!" or something retarded like that. Sometimes I'll say "Dyn-o-mite" just to humor him, but my heart's not in it. Do you know whose face is on the paper money in China? If you guessed Mao, you're not even close—it's Scott Baio circa *Charles in Charge.*

My biggest fear, the one that keeps me up nights, is that American soldiers are going to pour over the demilitarized zone, seize all of North Korea's television transmitters and start broadcasting that show with Jim Belushi in it. I sleep with a gun by my pillow, and if that ever happens, yours truly is putting a bullet in his head.

RALPH NADER CONSIDERS WRECKING 2004 ELECTION

But Prominent Crackpots Are Cool to Bid

Activist Ralph Nader is considering wrecking the 2004 presidential election, carrying on an election-wrecking tradition he began in 2000, associates of the spoiler said today.

Mr. Nader was huddling with prominent crackpots in Washington, D.C., today to determine whether he has enough support among wing-nuts and whack-jobs nationwide to mount an entirely meaningless campaign.

"If I wreck the 2004 election, I intend to wreck it in all fifty states," Mr. Nader told reporters today. "I have no intention of being merely a regional spoiler."

Mr. Nader added: "If you're going to screw up an election, screw it up big-time. My supporters expect nothing less from me."

But across the country, significant numbers of crackpots who have supported Mr. Nader in the past appeared to be cool to his latest bid to wreck the 2004 election.

"If I'm going to waste my vote, I want to be sure I'm wasting it on the right banana-head," said longtime crackpot Harlan Brill, who supported Rep. Dennis Kucinich (D-Ohio) in this week's Delaware primary. "It is time for Ralph Nader to step aside for a new generation of goofballs."

For his part, Mr. Nader said that he would "listen to the voices of crackpots everywhere" before making a final decision to screw up the 2004 race.

If he decides not to run, Mr. Nader said, he will actively seek out people who are in the middle of *The Da Vinci Code* and wreck the ending for them.

"It won't be as satisfying as spoiling an entire election, but I think it will still be rewarding on some level," Mr. Nader said.

Many prominent crackpots want Ralph Nader (above) to step aside for a new generation of egomaniacal goofballs.

EXPERTS GIVE THUMBS-UP TO FIRST-COUSIN MARRIAGES; HILLBILLIES, BRITISH ROYAL FAMILY JUBILANT

State of Kentucky Declares Official Day of Celebration

One day after experts announced that marriages between first cousins were significantly less risky than had previously been thought, jubilant cousin-fanciers praised the findings as a major step forward for inbreeders everywhere.

Reaction to the news was especially joyous in the state of Kentucky, which will celebrate the findings with an official state holiday, tentatively called Kissin' Cousins Day.

Elsewhere, exuberant hillbillies relished what many of them saw as a vindication of their inbreeding lifestyle.

"I'm just relieved that I won't have to lie about meeting my wife in high school anymore," said Dirk Wesson of Slug Hollow, West Virginia.

Amid the general euphoria, however, there was some carping in the hillbilly community that it took scientists so long to jump on the inbreeding bandwagon.

"We were ahead of the curve on this one," said Clem McGillicutty, a noted hillbilly and prominent inbreeding advocate. "Wonder how long it'll take those so-called 'experts' to recognize the health benefits of grain alcohol?"

Prince Charles (pictured) reacts to the news that first-cousin marriages carry few genetic risks.

On the other side of the Atlantic, a spokesman for the British royal family said that the Windsors were "pinching themselves" about the inbreeding developments.

"It's jolly good news," said Charles, the Prince of Wales. "It certainly opens up a fellow's options a bit, dating-wise."

Prince Charles has long been linked with British aristocrat Camilla Parker Bowles, but the new, bullish findings about inbreeding seemed to put a question mark over that relationship.

"All bets are off now," said Prince Charles. "I feel like a chap in a candy store."

SEGWAY CREATOR INVENTS "ROUND THINGY"

Amazing New Invention Shrouded in Secrecy

Inventor Dean Kamen, who just six months ago created the Segway—a scooter unlike any scooter the world had ever seen—has done it again, this time inventing a "round thingy" that will revolutionize transportation.

Sources close to Kamen say that the round thingy—so shrouded in secrecy that it is referred to in its patent filing only as "the round thingy"—could be attached by means of an axle to other round thingies for use on cars, buses, trucks and other vehicles.

"When people see Dean's round thingy in action, it is absolutely going to rock their world," one associate of Mr. Kamen said.

Critics of Mr. Kamen, however, were more skeptical of the Kamen camp's claims for its amazing new round thingy.

"Dean Kamen isn't the only person in the world who's been trying to develop a round thingy," said Dr. Louis Peverall of the Massachusetts Institute of Technology. "The question is whether his round thingy will succeed where so many other round thingies have failed."

Mr. Kamen, unfazed by the critics, is poised to unveil a series of other groundbreaking inventions in addition to his astonishing round thingy.

His new inventions include a writing implement fabricated from a sharpened piece of graphite encased in wood; an amazing lighting

Segway creator Dean Kamen has been evasive on the subject of his latest invention, which he calls a "round thingy."

device that consists of an electrified filament contained in an airtight glass bulb; and a hand-held, gear-driven kitchen tool for the "beating" of eggs.

TIM RUSSERT PLANNING TO USE ANNOYING CHALKBOARD ON ELECTION NIGHT AGAIN, NBC EXECS FEAR

Newsman, Irritating Prop Have Been "Inseparable" Since Election 2000

NBC newsman Tim Russert, who used a small, handheld chalkboard to illustrate various Electoral College calculations on Election Night 2000, plans to use the annoying prop again this Tuesday night, network insiders worry.

"That chalkboard of Tim's was cute at first," one NBC news executive said today. "But ever since the 2000 election, Tim's been carrying it around everywhere he goes. I mean, get over it."

Other executives agreed, saying Mr. Russert and his chalkboard have been "inseparable" since the lame prop made its debut in 2000.

According to one news executive, Mr. Russert brings the chalkboard with him to NBC staff meetings and uses it to tally up how many good points he makes, as well as how many stupid remarks are made by others.

"He has one column on the chalkboard labeled GOOD, and one labeled STUPID, and he's always making these little chalk marks when you're trying to say something," the executive

Tim Russert's annoying little chalkboard has worn out its welcome, coworkers say.

said. "Tim and his little chalkboard have turned into one gigantic pain in the ass, and I'm not the only one who feels that way."

In other election coverage news, the three major networks announced today that they have agreed to wait until the polls are closed before incorrectly predicting the winner of a tight congressional race.

"Once we have confirmation that the polls have closed, then and only then will we incorrectly announce that the loser won the race," CBS anchor Dan Rather said.

GOD, GOOGLED, EXISTS

59,900,000 Search Results Evidence of Deity, Experts Agree

In the most conclusive evidence of a Supreme Being ever discovered, a Google™ search of God has proved once and for all that He exists, theologians agreed today.

"To those doubters out there who still don't believe that God exists, I have just one piece of advice: Google™ Him," said Dr. George Darlington of the University of Minnesota Divinity School.

The Google™ search of God turned up over 59 million websites featuring Him, a number that theological scholars around the world said makes God's existence an open and shut case.

The stunning discovery, expected to wipe out atheism worldwide, was made entirely by accident by Jason Blivens, 22, a video-store clerk in Tacoma, Washington.

Speaking to reporters today at his home, Mr. Blivens said he meant to do a Google™ search of the word "bod" but accidentally typed the letter "g" instead of "b."

"As soon as those search results came up, I immediately alerted the authorities," Mr. Blivens said. "I knew this was something big."

In contrast with the 59 million sites found for God, a Google™ for Satan turned up only 3 million sites, suggesting that God is much more powerful than Satan, as theologians have long argued.

But in a finding that some scholars called worrisome, Paris Hilton turned up on over 3.5 million sites, indicating that the hotel heiress has actually eclipsed the Lord of Darkness as a force for evil.

In a positive development, however, "good" received 178 million search results while "evil" snagged only 17 million, 16 million of those stemming from foreign policy speeches by President George W. Bush.

LET THERE BE SITES: The Almighty racks up impressive Google™ stats.

STEINBRENNER BUYS FENWAY PARK

Homeless Red Sox Cry Foul

George Steinbrenner's buying spree continued unabated today as the New York Yankees owner purchased Fenway Park, the legendary home of the archrival Boston Red Sox.

In buying Fenway out from under the Sox, Mr. Steinbrenner has left his Eastern Division rivals without a stadium for the first time in their history, jeopardizing the Red Sox's bid for the American League pennant.

"It is hard to win a championship without pitching or hitting," said David Hastings, a sports historian at the University of Minnesota. "But it is virtually impossible to win without a stadium."

Red Sox owner John Henry, who spent most of the day scrambling to find a high school sandlot where his team might play the 2004 season, held an emotional press conference in Boston to denounce the big-spending Yankee honcho.

"Damn you, George Steinbrenner, damn you!" swore Mr. Henry, shaking his fist violently.

But Mr. Steinbrenner's shopping day had barely begun, as he went on to outbid the Walt Disney Company for the legendary puppet characters the Muppets.

While Mr. Steinbrenner did not indicate what role the Muppet characters might play in the Yankee organization, his aggressive purchase of Kermit, Miss Piggy et al. reinforced the impression in baseball circles that the Yankee owner is

Yankee owner George Steinbrenner's decision to buy Fenway Park has left the Boston Red Sox without a home for the first time in franchise history.

willing to buy anything that is not nailed down.

Having assumed the $250 million contract of third baseman Alex Rodriguez, however, Mr. Steinbrenner acknowledged that he might have to economize by outsourcing second base to India.

In other baseball news, North Korea's Kim Jong Il revealed that he attempted to acquire A-Rod until he was told that A-Rod was not a piece of nuclear fuel.

SADDAM'S TRIAL SET FOR MODESTO

Blunts Economic Impact of Losing Peterson Case, Locals Say

Despite mounting protests from Iraqi Shiites demanding that the U.S. turn over Saddam Hussein to them for trial, interim administrator Paul Bremer III announced today that the former Iraqi dictator would be put on trial this spring in Modesto, California.

"We needed to find a place where jurors were likely to give Saddam a fair trial," Mr. Bremer explained to reporters. "In Modesto, almost no one has heard of Saddam because the only news they have been getting for the last year has been about Scott Peterson."

In contrast with the Shiites, who took to the streets to protest the decision, Modesto residents were jubilant at the prospect of hosting the high-profile trial, especially after losing the Peterson trial to San Mateo County.

"The economic impact of losing the Scott Peterson case was devastating," said Ryan McCoy, who owns a café in downtown Modesto and sells gallons of Evian water to visiting journalists. "That's why it's such a good thing that we got Saddam—whoever he is."

But even as Modesto residents celebrated landing the Iraqi madman's trial, legal experts worried that locals here may not know enough about Saddam Hussein to sit on his jury, with many prospective jurors believing that Saddam was somehow implicated in the Peterson case.

When asked the question, "Who is Saddam Hussein?" Modesto resident Jan Clarke, 35, gave a typical response: "Is he the guy who rented the boat to Scott?"

In Baghdad, Mr. Bremer said the U.S. was exploring a number of scenarios to compensate the angry Shiites for the loss of Saddam, including moving Michael Jackson's trial to the southern city of Basra.

Sound trucks are at the ready for Saddam Hussein's much-anticipated trial in Modesto, California.

NORTH KOREA EXPELS IRAN FROM AXIS OF EVIL; NO LONGER EVIL ENOUGH, SAYS KIM

Looking for "Evillerdoer," North Korean Says

One day after Iran agreed to put a halt to its nuclear program in response to pressure from the international community, North Korea expelled Iran from the Axis of Evil, saying that Iran was "no longer evil enough."

The decision to oust Iran was made unilaterally by North Korean dictator Kim Jong Il, who aides said was "hopping mad" at Iran's decision to abide by the anti-nuke mandate.

"You call yourself evildoers?" a furious Kim reportedly bellowed into the phone when he received a call from Iran's Foreign Minister Kamal Kharrazi, notifying him of Iran's decision to comply. "My sharpei is eviller than you!"

The expulsion of Iran is just the latest blow to the Axis of Evil, long considered the most elite club of evildoers in the world.

The AOE already lost one of its founding members, Iraq, with the fall of Iraqi madman Saddam Hussein in April, making the departure of Iran potentially devastating to the evil consortium.

As a result, Mr. Kim has shifted into recruitment mode, looking for what he called an "evillerdoer" or two who could join the Axis of Evil and bring it back up to full strength.

Iranian soldiers bid a fond farewell to the Axis of Evil just hours after being dismissed by a furious Kim Jong Il of North Korea.

On Mr. Kim's short list, aides say, are the nation of Syria and the singer-actress Liza Minnelli, who yesterday was accused of beating up her ex-husband, David Gest, during their brief but tempestuous union.

Elsewhere, in a Pentagon memo released today, Secretary of Defense Donald H. Rumsfeld writes that there is no way of knowing what, if any, progress has been made in the war against Condoleezza Rice.

KIM'S BLOG

The Axis of Evil was a cool idea in the beginning—get the most evil nations in the world together around a table and see if we could do bigger, better evil things by working as a unit than we could if we were out on our own. At the very least, I thought, it was a chance to share some basic things like mailing lists.

Somewhere along the line, though, things went horribly wrong. I know, it's time for me to stop bitching about Iraq and Iran dropping out of the Axis—it's time for me to move on, and find new, truly evil Axis members.

One thing I've decided, though—after getting burned by Iraq and Iran, I'm going to make double-damn sure that any evildoers who want to join the AOE in the future have "the right stuff" to be a member in good standing. To that end, I've devised the following "Axis of Evil Aptitude Test."

1. When you see a little old lady crossing the street, do you:
(a) help her across?
(b) run for your life?
(c) remove a manhole cover and give her a swift kick in the ass?

2. What words best describe you?
(a) thoughtful and caring
(b) works well with others
(c) the devil incarnate

3. If you won Superlotto or Powerball, would you:
(a) retire to the South of France
(b) create a charitable foundation to stamp out poverty
(c) plow it all into spent nuclear fuel rods and torture chambers

If you answered "c" to the above questions, please send your résumé to: sexybeast@axisofevil.org. Peace out!

KERRY BASHES DEAN'S HEAD AGAINST HOOD OF CAR

Hot-Tempered Dems in Parking-Lot Free-for-All

The hotly contested Iowa race reached the boiling point today as Sen. John Kerry (D-Mass.) repeatedly bashed former Vermont Governor Howard Dean's head against the hood of a car in a Davenport parking lot.

The violent incident occurred outside the town hall after a candidates' forum and may have been ignited by what was described as a "taunting dance" performed by Mr. Dean.

The former Vermont Governor, giddy with the endorsement of former rival Ambassador Carol Moseley Braun, was doing an "end-zone boogie" for Mr. Kerry's benefit when the Massachusetts senator blew his stack.

With Sen. Edward M. Kennedy (D-Mass.) pinning Mr. Dean's arms, Mr. Kerry started bashing the frontrunner's head against the hood of a parked Saturn.

"I've had just about enough of you, Howard!" Mr. Kerry reportedly thundered.

Within moments, Rep. Dennis Kucinich (D-Ohio) appeared, jumping on Mr. Kerry's back and pulling him off Mr. Dean, provoking the remaining Democratic contenders to join the fray.

Mark Newton, a parking-lot attendant who witnessed the fight, said, "Gephardt was fighting like a girl, slapping and all. It made me think twice about voting for him."

Reached in New Hampshire, retired General Wesley Clark told reporters, "This is why I skipped Iowa. I had a feeling something like this would happen."

But parking-lot attendant Newton expressed the view of many Democrats in Iowa when he said he was "disappointed" by the violent free-for-all.

"These guys finally do something worth watching, and it's not even on TV," he said.

Democratic presidential candidate Howard Dean's steady stream of sarcastic remarks may have sparked Sen. John Kerry's parking-lot rampage.

SCHWARZENEGGER ORDERS BREAST IMPLANT INSPECTIONS

Names Self Inspector-in-Chief

Calling silicone breast implants "the biggest problem facing California today," Governor Arnold Schwarzenegger today ordered mandatory silicone breast implant inspections for every woman in California.

"The time has come to say '*hasta la vista*' to fake breasts," Governor Schwarzenegger said, introducing a bill calling for silicone inspection teams to fan out across the state.

With a towering budget deficit plaguing California, many observers in Sacramento were surprised that Mr. Schwarzenegger would name fake breasts the most worrisome problem on his agenda.

But the Governor today declared his commitment to cracking down on what he called California's "fake breast epidemic," naming himself California's "breast inspector-in-chief."

Mr. Schwarzenegger then led a team of breast inspectors through southern California's San Fernando Valley, which the Governor has derided as "Silicone Valley" in recent speeches.

Wearing a baseball cap reading FAKE BREAST INSPECTOR #1, Governor Schwarzenegger pounded on doors, shouting, "This is your Governor! Show me your breasts!" causing many residents to bolt their doors and phone the authorities.

While opposition groups howled that the fake-breast-implant-inspection regime was im-

proper and might even be unconstitutional, the Governor remained undaunted.

"We just need more time," Mr. Schwarzenegger said. "The inspections are working."

HASTA LA VISTA TO IMPLANTS: California Governor Arnold Schwarzenegger vows to have a hands-on role in the state's ambitious program of breast implant inspections.

INTERROGATORS SHOW SADDAM "TRISTA AND RYAN'S WEDDING"

Rumsfeld Defends Tactics

U.S. interrogators are pressuring Saddam Hussein to cooperate with them by repeatedly showing him ABC's two-hour wedding special featuring *Bachelorette*'s Trista Rehn and Ryan Sutter, the Pentagon acknowledged today.

News of the Pentagon's use of "Trista and Ryan's Wedding" rippled through international human rights circles today, with some watchdog groups claiming that showing certain reality programs to prisoners of war could be in violation of the Geneva Conventions.

"Watching Trista marry Ryan once is punishment, but watching it six, seven times in a row may in fact constitute torture," said Dr. Josef Claire, a leading human rights activist based in Brussels.

At a press briefing in Washington, Secretary of Defense Donald H. Rumsfeld said that showing Saddam the video of the Rehn-Sutter nuptials was "something we did not enter into lightly."

"Is forcing someone to watch 'Trista and Ryan's Wedding' cruel? Yes," Mr. Rumsfeld said. "But I submit to you: so is Saddam Hussein."

In addition to defending the use of the excruciating wedding special, the Defense Secretary refused to rule out playing Clay Aiken's new CD to the Iraqi madman "over and over again until he screams."

Images like this may be used to "torture" former Iraqi President Saddam Hussein, human rights activists fear.

"If I may remind you, gentlemen," he said, "we are at war."

In other Saddam news, the owner of the farm in Tikrit where the Iraqi strongman was captured objected to the media's characterization of the dictator's hiding place as a "hole."

"You try to rent out a place that everybody and his uncle is calling a hole," the farmer said. "Okay, it's not roomy, but it would be perfect for a young couple starting out."

TREASURY SECRETARY RIPPED FOR "FRIGGIN' BANANA REPUBLIC" REMARKS

White House Apologizes for O'Neill's Ricky Ricardo Imitation

Continuing his difficult tour of Latin America, Treasury Secretary Paul O'Neill apologized to Argentina's President Eduardo Duhalde today for remarks in which O'Neill called Argentina "a friggin' banana republic."

Secretary O'Neill's controversial comments, made to reporters as his plane touched down in Argentina, were as follows: "Lend money to Argentina? No way! I'm not giving one thin dime to that friggin' banana republic."

Mr. O'Neill later characterized the remarks as "insensitive" and offered the cash-strapped Latin American nation $30 billion in loan guarantees to make amends.

But right after his meeting with President Duhalde, the Treasury Secretary turned to reporters and said, "Well, that's thirty bill down the drain. I'll bet old Duhalde just goes out dancing with a bowl of fruit on his head."

After his bowl-of-fruit remarks created a furor in Latin American circles, Secretary O'Neill apologized once again and granted Argentina another $30 billion worth of loan relief.

But upon boarding the plane to leave Argentina, Mr. O'Neill fanned the flames of controversy yet again, saying he did a "killer

Treasury Secretary Paul O'Neill's overactive piehole may have cost taxpayers billions during his recent Latin American tour, administration insiders worry.

imitation" of President Duhalde, launching into a performance reminiscent of a hotheaded tirade by the Ricky Ricardo character on the old *I Love Lucy* television series.

By the time the day was over, the U.S. had pledged over $90 billion in loan guarantees to Argentina to apologize for Mr. O'Neill's various missteps, leaving many White House aides frustrated by the Treasury Secretary's penchant for costly faux pas.

"Every time O'Neill opens his piehole, it costs the taxpayers another thirty billion dollars," one aide groused.

POLL: SOCCER MOMS FEEL TAKEN FOR GRANTED BY NASCAR DADS

NASCAR Dads Accuse Soccer Moms of "Nagging"

According to a survey of two key constituencies in the 2004 presidential race, soccer moms feel that they are being "taken for granted" by NASCAR dads, while NASCAR dads wish that soccer moms would "stop their nagging already."

The poll, conducted by the Crandall Public Opinion Institute at the University of Minnesota, shows that 70 percent of soccer moms agree with the statement, "These NASCAR dads are not the NASCAR dads we married."

Additionally, 63 percent of the soccer moms feel that NASCAR dads are spending "too much time" being courted by presidential candidates and "not enough time" performing such basic household tasks as carpooling, taking out the garbage, and raking leaves.

For their part, 82 percent of NASCAR dads surveyed in the poll said they had had "just about enough" of the soccer moms' complaining.

Even more tellingly, 100 percent agreed with the statement "I would rather go to a NASCAR race than sit around listening to this crap."

Ominously, an equal percentage of soccer moms agreed with the statement "Fine, but don't expect me to be here when you get back."

Dr. David Givens, who conducted the survey for the University of Minnesota, said that soccer moms may once again mobilize as a political force in 2004, but added, "There's an equal chance that they may just go home to their mothers."

Warning that "hell hath no fury like a soccer mom scorned," Dr. Givens said that the soccer moms' anger at the NASCAR dads may wind up benefiting two other key constituencies, handsome pool men and cable installers.

NAG, NAG, NAG: Relations between soccer moms (pictured, above) and NASCAR dads have never been more strained.

ASHCROFT URGES MILITARY TRIBUNAL FOR WHITE HOUSE TURKEY

No Pardon for Gitmo-Bound Poultry

U.S. Attorney General John Ashcroft pressed President Bush to withhold the customary pre-Thanksgiving pardon for the White House turkey today, forcefully arguing that the bird should face a military tribunal at Camp X-Ray in Guantánamo, Cuba.

FBI agents arrested the turkey moments before the traditional pardoning ceremony, taking it away in shackles as a busload of third-graders watched in horror.

The decision to detain the White House turkey at Gitmo surprised many in Washington who had expected the turkey to receive leniency from Mr. Bush.

But in a press conference at the Justice Department, Mr. Ashcroft said that there were "too many questions" hovering over the suspicious poultry to let it go free.

"We would very much like to know how he got on the White House lawn and what he intended to do while he was there," Mr. Ashcroft said.

The Attorney General added that, using powers granted by the Patriot Act, the Justice Department had placed the fowl under surveillance over eight months ago, eavesdropping on the turkey's conversations and following its movements on a twenty-four-hour basis.

Justice Department officials seize the White House turkey, which was later sent to Camp X-Ray in Guantánamo, Cuba.

Mr. Ashcroft said that the Justice Department pounced on the turkey after noticing an increase in "suspicious chatter" from the bird over the past seventy-two hours.

"While I'm sure some would argue that it was merely innocuous gobbling, we were not prepared to take that risk," Mr. Ashcroft said.

Mr. Ashcroft used his press conference to wish all Americans a happy Thanksgiving, adding, "I may not be sitting at the same table as you, but I'll be listening."

IN POLICY SHIFT, U.S. PUTS IRAQ ON EBAY

No Takers in First 24 Hours

In what was seen as a marked shift in American foreign policy, on Sunday the U.S. put the entire nation of Iraq up for sale on the Internet auction site eBay.

The decision to list the Middle Eastern nation on the popular auction site surprised many at the United Nations, where just days ago President George W. Bush had made an impassioned plea for troops and money to help rebuild the war-torn country.

But Mr. Bush hinted at the policy shift in his national radio address Saturday, saying, "We are not occupiers nor liberators: we are highly motivated sellers."

French President Jacques Chirac was the first to notice the listing of Iraq on eBay Sunday morning, when the French leader logged on in search of some rare Edith Piaf recordings.

While surfing the auction site, Mr. Chirac noticed the listing for the oil-rich nation, with an asking price of $87 billion and a seller identified only as RUMMY55.

Jake Braswell, 39, a video-store clerk who regularly visits eBay in search of memorabilia from the seventies television series *Battlestar Gallactica*, said he had no intention of putting in a bid for Iraq, adding that he thought the listing itself was "misleading."

"No way is Iraq in 'mint condition,'" Mr. Braswell said.

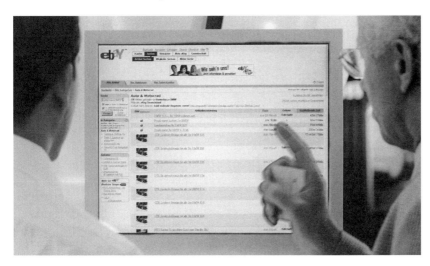

Iraq has seen few takers since being listed on eBay, the White House confirmed.

101

ACE OF DIAMONDS IRKED BY NO. 4 RANKING

Calls Uday, Qusay "Do-Nothings"

Abid Hamid Mahmud al-Tikriti, the just-captured "ace of diamonds" from the former Iraqi regime of Saddam Hussein, last night blasted his number-four status, arguing that he should rank higher than both Uday and Qusay Hussein in the infamous deck of cards.

"When the Americans told me I was number four, I practically fell out of my chair," Mr. Mahmud told CNN's Larry King during an hour-long interview. "What were they smoking when they put together these rankings?"

Mr. Mahmud attempted to portray himself as a victim of nepotism, claiming that the Hussein sons' role in Saddam's brutal dictatorship had been "blown way out of proportion" and that the two aces were "do-nothings."

"So Uday goes and steals a billion dollars from an Iraqi bank," Mr. Mahmud said. "Larry, when you're one of Saddam's sons, that's like making a trip to an ATM."

As for Qusay Hussein, Mr. Mahmud offered an even more withering portrayal.

"As far as I can remember, Qusay spent all his time at the Presidential Palace playing with his Sony PlayStation and downloading movies over the Internet," Mr. Mahmud said. "If he's an ace, then I'm Scooby-Doo."

Less than an hour after Mr. Mahmud's controversial interview was broadcast, former Iraqi strongman Saddam Hussein came out swinging in defense of his sons on *Access Hollywood.*

"There's always a whiner in every organization, and in our brutal dictatorship that was definitely Mahmud," Saddam said. "He's still mad that Qusay beat him out for Employee of the Month last November."

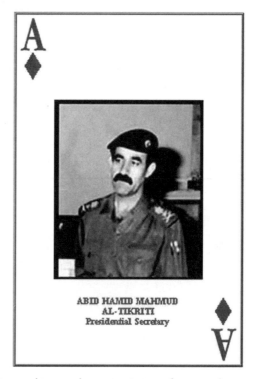

ABID HAMID MAHMUD
AL-TIKRITI
Presidential Secretary

Among his complaints, Iraq's Ace of Diamonds says his face card makes him look "like a goon."

SUPREME COURT OVERTURNS GORE'S ENDORSEMENT OF DEAN

Transfers Nod to Bush in 5–4 Decision

Just moments after former Vice President Al Gore endorsed former Vermont Governor Howard Dean for President in Harlem yesterday, the Supreme Court overturned his endorsement by a 5–4 margin.

The Court, finding the former Vice President's endorsement of Mr. Dean unconstitutional, transferred his endorsement to President George W. Bush instead.

Writing for the majority, Chief Justice William Rehnquist said, "There's really no explanation necessary—we're the Supreme Court, and if you don't like it, you can stick it where the moon don't shine."

While some Democrats howled that the Court was inappropriately politicizing itself with its controversial decision, Mr. Gore accepted the ruling, saying, "After four minutes of partisan wrangling over this matter, it is time for us to move on."

Mr. Gore expressed some regret that his endorsement had been transferred from Mr. Dean to Mr. Bush, but added, "It'll be nice to be on the winning side for a change."

The Supreme Court's decision to overturn Al Gore's endorsement of Howard Dean by a 5–4 margin stirred fresh controversy in Washington.

But Mr. Gore's endorsement could turn out to be a mixed blessing for the Bush campaign, as a survey of those who heard Mr. Gore's Harlem speech showed that 55 percent felt "drowsy," while 40 percent "lost consciousness altogether."

In other news from the White House, President Bush said today that he was determined to find the person or persons responsible for leaking the similarities between Iraq and Vietnam, and reminded the press that Iraq, in his words, was "much sandier."

SOLAR FLARE BRIEFLY KNOCKS OUT STING'S EGO

Impact on Singer Expected To Be Temporary, Scientists Say

A gigantic solar flare slammed into the Earth's magnetic field on Wednesday morning, briefly knocking out the ego of singer-actor Sting, scientists said.

The performer was promoting his new book, a memoir entitled *Broken Music*, on the television program *Live with Regis and Kelly*, when the solar flare slammed into the Earth's magnetic field.

Sting had begun telling the program's co-hosts about how his lifelong love affair with music began, when he suddenly stopped, mid-sentence.

"Oh, who the bloody hell cares?" Sting said, the audience gasping as he tossed his book aside in apparent disgust.

It was only hours later that scientists determined that the former Police front man's loss of ego, believed to be temporary in nature, had been caused by the solar flare, surprising many experts.

"We had thought that the solar flare would have an effect on satellite and cellular phone transmissions," said Dr. Kenneth Reid, a solar flare expert at the University of Minnesota's Clausen Observatory. "We had no idea that it was powerful enough to knock out Sting's ego."

Elsewhere, associates of the pop singer and

The ego of Sting (above) was expected to make a full recovery.

MTV star Jessica Simpson said that the solar flare might have caused Ms. Simpson's brain to function temporarily.

Moments after the flare hit the Earth's magnetic field, Ms. Simpson was observed correctly identifying canned tuna and brushing her teeth without assistance.

Ms. Simpson's behavior was an "aberration," Dr. Reid said, and she was expected to be back to bumping into doors and walls within hours.

DAVID BLAINE TO GO 44 DAYS WITHOUT PUBLICITY

Boldest Stunt Yet for Master Magician

Internationally renowned magician David Blaine stunned the world today by announcing that for his next stunt he would attempt to go forty-four days without publicity.

A spokesman for the master illusionist confirmed that, commencing November 1, Mr. Blaine would go forty-four days "without generating headlines, appearing in TV specials, or being photographed in New York nightclubs with German supermodels."

While some in the world of magic and illusion called Mr. Blaine's audacious new stunt his boldest ever, others doubted that he could pull it off.

Dr. Randall Kendrick, an adjunct professor at the University of Minnesota who teaches a graduate course in the history of celebrity magicians, is among the doubters.

"It is important to remember that, in addition to being a magician, Mr. Blaine is a celebrity," Dr. Kendrick says. "Celebrities can go without a lot of things for forty-four days—carbs, for example—but publicity is not one of them."

Dr. Kendrick points to the example of on-again, off-again lovebirds Jennifer Lopez and Ben Affleck, who canceled their wedding after complaining about the overwhelming crush of publicity, only to be photographed procuring a gun license together a few days later, making tabloid headlines around the world.

"By most estimates, J. Lo and Ben were able to go approximately thirty-six hours without publicity," Dr. Kendrick says. "I'd be surprised if David Blaine holds out much longer than that."

In other news, the State of Illinois announced today that it would start buying drugs from Canada, while the State of Ohio confirmed that it would start sleeping with Sweden.

If magician David Blaine (pictured) is to succeed in going forty-four days without publicity, he may have to put his shirt back on, experts say.

MANY HALLIBURTON EXECS STILL WITHOUT EVIAN

Cheney Urges Patience

One month after the conclusion of the active combat phase of the war in Iraq, many Halliburton executives stationed in that country are still without Evian water and other basic necessities, a spokesman for the executives said today.

"We have been promised Evian for weeks, but so far that has been an empty promise," said Kenneth Barber, the Halliburton spokesman. "It

Halliburton executives stationed in Iraq have been without Evian for weeks, the company confirmed today.

is time for the U.S. to back up its words with actions."

Mr. Barber said that weeks ago, a representative of interim administrator L. Paul Bremer asked the Halliburton employees what kind of water they preferred—"sparkling or still."

"That was the last we heard from him," Mr. Barber said. "How long could it take for him to come back with our water?"

Mr. Barber said that the absence of Evian water could set off a humanitarian crisis among the Halliburton executives, many of whom have already gone weeks without Starbucks coffee or flaky croissants.

In a speech to the people of Halliburton, Vice President Dick Cheney urged the increasingly unhappy executives to be "patient."

"We know that the pace of reconstruction has been slow, but soon Iraq will be full of four-star restaurants and gourmet takeout places that will be the envy of the region," Mr. Cheney said.

Meanwhile, the Bush administration announced a "major victory" in the search for Saddam's weapons of mass destruction as it uncovered what it called "a fully operational Botox facility" in Beverly Hills, California.

The White House said that U.S. forces seized significant quantities of Botox and the actress Goldie Hawn.

U.S. DEMANDS EXPLANATION OF WHO BECKHAM IS

Increased Beckham-Related Chatter Has State Department on Edge

The U.S., deluged in recent weeks by press reports and television appearances by someone named "Beckham," has demanded that the British government offer a "full explanation of exactly who this Beckham person is," the State Department said today.

"We are not sure what he is famous for, but we would like to know who he is and why exactly we are being forced to care about him all of a sudden," Secretary of State Colin Powell told reporters in a press briefing today.

While concerns about a sharp uptick in Beckham-related chatter had already put many at the State Department on edge, Beckham's appearance with his wife Posh Spice at last week's MTV Movie Awards raised the State Department's anxiety to the boiling point.

"In addition to explaining who exactly Beckham is, we are asking the British government to remind us who Posh Spice is again," Mr. Powell said.

While relations between Britain and the U.S. have never been warmer, their close ties could be torn asunder by their differences over Beckham, experts fear.

"In America, almost no one knows who Beckham is, while in Britain, he is considered the most famous person on the planet," said Dr.

One of these people is believed to be David Beckham, the State Department said.

Roger Cranepool of the Institute for Foreign Relations at the University of Minnesota. "This is a recipe for disaster."

In his press briefing, Secretary Powell also put pressure on Britain's Tony Blair to explain the title of the recent British film *Bend It Like Beckham.*

"Not only do we have no idea who Beckham is, we have no idea what 'bending it' is," Mr. Powell said.

AHMED CHALABI BLOWS TELEVISED IRAQI TRIVIA QUIZ

Misspells "Baghdad" on National TV

Disgraced Iraqi National Congress leader Ahmed Chalabi, formerly the Pentagon's first choice to run the government of the new Iraq, attempted to worm his way back into the Iraqi people's hearts by appearing last night on a nationally televised Iraqi trivia quiz.

The telecast, which Mr. Chalabi orchestrated with the aid of Iranian agents to demonstrate his fitness to lead Iraq, began with a seemingly confident Chalabi telling the program's host that he was "totally stoked" about having his Iraqi trivia knowledge put to the test.

Mr. Chalabi started the contest strongly, answering the first question, "What is the capital of Iraq?" with a confident "Baghdad."

After the host told Mr. Chalabi he had answered the question correctly, Mr. Chalabi responded with an exuberant "Yes!" and pumped his fist in the air.

But when the host asked the next question—"How do you spell 'Baghdad'?"—the Iraqi exile, who until last year had been out of the country for forty-five years, tensed noticeably.

Mr. Chalabi proceeded to spell "Baghdad" haltingly, omitting the crucial "h."

"I'm sorry," the host said. "That was a tricky one."

Mr. Chalabi's performance worsened from there, as the long-exiled Iraqi missed such crucial pieces of Iraqi trivia as the nation's neigh-

Ahmed Chalabi's poor performance during the "lightning round" of a nationally televised Iraqi trivia quiz may put a damper on the former exile's political aspirations.

bors, major products and official bird.

After the broadcast, Secretary of Defense Donald Rumsfeld said that the show had served at least one purpose, in that it had given the U.S. yet another opportunity to ransack Mr. Chalabi's house while he was on TV.

KIM JONG IL PLANNING TO BRING ENORMOUS NUCLEAR BOMB TO BEIJING SUMMIT

May Use Big Bomb as Bargaining Chip, State Department Fears

North Korean President Kim Jong Il threw a monkey wrench into plans for the upcoming nuclear summit between the U.S. and North Korea by announcing today that he plans to bring an enormous nuclear bomb with him to the Beijing meeting.

Mr. Kim, observers say, may believe that having an enormous nuclear bomb with him at the negotiating table could prove helpful as a bargaining chip in the upcoming talks.

Moments after the controversial announcement, U.S. officials worried aloud that by bringing a huge nuclear bomb with him to Beijing Mr. Kim could be endangering the summit's chances for success.

"If Kim Jong Il shows up in Beijing and there's a big nuclear bomb sitting next to him at that table, that could wreck everything," one State Department official said today.

While some at the State Department were hopeful that the mercurial Kim was merely bluffing, others noted with some concern that he had reserved a two-bedroom suite at the Beijing Marriott, accommodations large enough for both him and an enormous nuclear weapon.

At the White House, spokesman Ari Fleis-cher said that the move by Kim would not scuttle Secretary of State Colin Powell's appearance at the Beijing summit, but that Mr. Powell now intended to show up with an antiballistic missile system and three aircraft carriers.

Mr. Fleischer added that while war with Pyongyang was not inevitable, the Bush administration had just awarded a $16.2 billion contract to the Bechtel Group for the reconstruction of North Korea "just in case."

North Korea's Kim Jong Il confirms that he plans to bring an enormous, ticking nuclear bomb with him to the bargaining table this week.

RUMSFELD SEEN HOLDING GLOBE IN HANDS, CACKLING MANIACALLY

Defense Secretary Questions Use of Word "Cackling"

Secretary of Defense Donald H. Rumsfeld was seen running through the streets of Washington late Saturday night carrying a globe and "cackling maniacally," according to witnesses who saw Mr. Rumsfeld's startling behavior.

The Defense Secretary was first spotted making his way down Pennsylvania Avenue, witnesses said, and was said to be performing "some kind of a crazy jig."

"He was shouting 'The world is mine!' and just cackling his head off," said Jonah Braymer, a high school teacher from Duluth who was taking his history students on a tour of the nation's capital. "The kids were all pretty scared."

In an appearance Sunday on NBC's *Meet the Press*, Mr. Rumsfeld told host Tim Russert that he did in fact run down Pennsylvania Avenue carrying a globe, but denied that he was in any way "cackling."

"Cackling? Cackling? Goodness gracious be, all you have to do is laugh a little these days and every Gloomy Gus, Nervous Nelly and Henny Penny will say you're cackling like a maniac," Mr. Rumsfeld said, cackling.

Elsewhere, in what is being described as "a major step forward on Iraq's road to democracy," a team led by White House advisor Karl Rove arrived in Baghdad today to teach the Iraqi people how to make negative campaign ads.

Mr. Rove acknowledged that, since Saddam Hussein ran for President unopposed for twenty-four years, the Iraqis have no experience with the kind of below-the-belt attack ads that have been the hallmark of American democracy.

But Mr. Rove said that if negative campaign ads take hold in Iraq, the politics of personal destruction and character assassination could eventually blossom across the Middle East.

A cackling Donald Rumsfeld (above) minutes before he went on his terrifying spree.

U.S. MAY LAUNCH AIR STRIKES FROM J. LO'S ASS

Move Would Reduce Turkey's Role, Pentagon Says

The U.S. military is seriously considering launching air strikes against Iraq from Jennifer Lopez's ass, sources close to both the Pentagon and the singer-actress revealed today.

The plan to use Ms. Lopez's ass as a staging area for air sorties against Baghdad came as a surprise to many in the international community, since the U.S. had been engaged in protracted negotiations to base troops and weaponry in neighboring Turkey.

But sources close to the discussions regarding Ms. Lopez's ass said that launching air strikes from the platinum recording artist's backside afforded the U.S. greater flexibility than the Turkish scenario.

"Right now, we're looking at a situation where we need to pay thirty billion dollars to get Turkey to let us use its bases," one Pentagon source said today. "Everything would be so much simpler if we just used J. Lo's ass."

In Hollywood, where antiwar sentiments dominate, some observers were surprised that the popular singer-actress would lend her ass to any possible military strike against Iraq.

Additionally, her controversial decision fueled speculation about a possible rift between Ms. Lopez and fiancé Ben Affleck, who had ear-

Jennifer Lopez's ass (pictured) could be a much more reliable staging area for an air attack than Turkey, a Defense Department spokesman said.

lier opposed the use of his ass for military purposes.

But according to Hollywood talent agent Buddy Schlantz, Ms. Lopez has made a shrewd career move by allowing her ass to join President Bush's "coalition of the willing."

"If the United States succeeds in ousting Saddam Hussein, this move is going to take J. Lo's ass to a whole new level," Mr. Schlantz said.

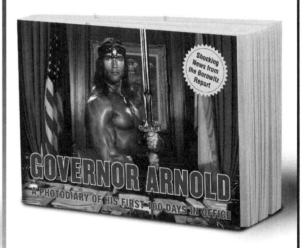